The Past
The Road from Isolation

About the Authors

Leon E. Clark, the author of *Through African Eyes*, is the general editor of the CITE World Culture Series. He received his B.A. and M.A. from Yale University and his doctorate in International Education from the University of Massachusetts. For the past fifteen years he has been involved in a variety of educational activities both within and outside the United States. He has been a high school and college teacher; Associate Director of the Social Sciences and Humanities Center, Teachers College, Columbia; and associate director of the Governmental Affairs Institute in Washington, D.C. He has also taught in the University of Mysore, India, conducted research in both India and Africa, and served as a consultant to several Asian and African nations. The author of several books and numerous articles on education and international affairs, Dr. Clark is presently on the faculty of American University in Washington, D.C.

Richard H. Minear is Professor of History at the University of Massachusetts in Amherst. He received his B.A. from Yale in 1960 and his Ph.D. in History and East Asian Languages from Harvard in 1968. During 1964-66 and again in 1970-71 he received Fulbright grants to live in Japan and conduct research on Japanese intellectual history. His publications include *Japanese Tradition and Western Law* (1970), *Victors' Justice: The Tokyo War Crimes Trial* (1971), and numerous articles for scholarly journals in the United States and abroad. All of his books and articles have been translated into Japanese.

THROUGH JAPANESE EYES

◄§ Volume 1

The Past
The Road from Isolation

RICHARD H. MINEAR

LEON E. CLARK, General Editor

A CITE BOOK

New York • Washington

Published in the United States of America in 1981
by The Center for International Training and Education
777 United Nations Plaza, New York, NY 10017

© 1974, 1981 by Leon E. Clark and Richard H. Minear

Library of Congress Catalog Card Number 81-67544

ISBN 0-938960-04-0

Printed in the United States of America

Contents

Foreword

PEOPLE—AND NATIONS—have a tendency to look at the outside world from their own perspectives. This is natural and perhaps necessary, for we are all prisoners of a particular space and time. But how limited and boring one perspective can be! And how faulty and biased our information would be if we listened only to ourselves!

The main goal of THROUGH JAPANESE EYES is to broaden our perspective by presenting a Japanese view of Japan and the world. Most of the material in these books has been written by Japanese, and it comes from a variety of sources: autobiographies, fiction, poetry, newspaper and magazine articles, letters, diaries, and historical documents.

Unlike most books about "other peoples," THROUGH JAPANESE EYES does not try to *explain* Japan but to *show* it; it does not offer "expert" analysis by outside observers but, rather, attempts to recreate the reality of everyday life as experienced by the Japanese people. Interpretation is left to the reader. In effect, THROUGH JAPANESE EYES has two objectives: to let the Japanese speak for themselves, and to let readers think for themselves.

Volume 1, *The Past: The Road from Isolation,* begins with a brief look at Japan as it is known to the world today: a nation of economic prosperity and technological excellence. It then goes back to the seventeenth century, to a time when Japan was isolated from the rest of the world, and traces some of the political and social developments that transformed this

hermit kingdom into a modern imperial power. Japan's contact
with the outside world led eventually to its involvement in
World War II, and the last third of this book examines some of
the causes of that war, its impact on the Japanese people, and
some of the permanent changes it brought about in Japan.

Volume 2, *The Present: Coping with Affluence*, focuses
on the personal, social, and environmental effects of Japan's
current prosperity. Like Europe and the United States, Japan
has discovered that affluence is a mixed blessing, bringing
water and air pollution and congested cities, along with material comforts and increased mobility. It also brings new life
styles. Much of the material in this book deals with contemporary Japanese attitudes toward women's roles, family
life, and religion. A final section is devoted to Japanese Americans, especially to their experiences in the United States during World War II.

Although Volume 2 is concerned primarily with contemporary issues, some historical selections are included to
provide continuity and contrast with the present.

In some ways, Japan may seem different from the United
States, and indeed it is. But in many more ways, the Japanese as
people are similar to people anywhere in the world. Human
beings, no matter where they live, face the same basic needs:
to eat, to work, to love, to play, to get along with their fellow
men. Learning how the Japanese respond to these needs may
teach us something useful for our own lives.

More important, getting to know the Japanese as people
—sharing in their thoughts and feelings, their beliefs and aspirations—should help us to develop a sense of empathy, a feeling of identity, with human beings everywhere. In the end we
should know more about ourselves—indeed, we should have an
expanded definition of who we are—because we will know
more about the common humanity that all people share. Self-
knowledge is the ultimate justification for studying about others.

LEON E. CLARK

The Past
The Road from Isolation

Introduction:
On Studying Japan

To MOST OF us today, Japan means very specific things: Honda and Yamaha motorcycles, Toyota and Datsun cars, Sony radios and tape recorders, Panasonic television sets, Nikon and Yashica cameras. To some of us, Japan means other things as well: Zen Buddhism, flower arrangement, World War II.

As vivid as these images are, they do not constitute anything like a complete or balanced picture of contemporary Japan. What is the scope of Japan's economic achievement today? Why is Japan the only highly industrialized society in Asia? What has success done to Japan and to the Japanese? Do they control their technology, or does it control them?

In Japan there is one television set for every four people, one car for every five people. In Tokyo one can buy Mac-Donald's hamburgers and Dunkin Donuts. And yet, the Japanese are very different from Americans. Or are they?

Through Japanese Eyes examines some of these questions and raises others. There are no easy answers, of course. But reading what the Japanese have to say about their own society should add an important dimension to our understanding of Japan.

In at least one sense, all people are alike. Japanese, Ameri-

cans, Chinese, Indians—all are confronted with the human condition, with man's fate: we are all born, we live, we die. But
the similarity between Japanese and Americans does not stop
there. Japanese and Americans today face many of the same
problems. Both peoples live in highly industrialized societies.
Both have achieved material prosperity. Both find themselves
asking what material prosperity means. So in reading about
Japan we find ourselves reflecting on our own society and on
ourselves.

The first section of this volume deals with Japan's affluence today, with the scope of Japan's economic success and the
ways in which it is changing the lives of individual Japanese.

We then move to a consideration of Japan's past. In the
seventeenth century—recent history by Japanese standards—
Japan was a closed society, sealed off from contact with the
rest of the world. The Japanese were proud of their heritage,
ready to assert that it was better than any other. We examine
the values of "premodern" Japan and find some values that
seem to be of great usefulness in building a modern society.

The middle of the nineteenth century brought radical
changes, transforming Japan from a hermit kingdom to an imperial power. How did the Japanese see their society? How did
others see Japan?

World War II then takes center stage. (For many of your
parents and grandparents, World War II is *the* thing that
comes to mind when Japan is mentioned.) We see the war and
Japan's defeat through the eyes of a fifteen-year-old Japanese
boy. The United States dropped atomic bombs on Hiroshima
and Nagasaki. We learn how a Japanese teenager reacted to
the bombing. Japan's wartime leader was Tojo Hideki,* the
Prime Minister. After the war he was tried and executed. What
kind of man was he? What were his goals?

Defeat in World War II led to major transformations in
Japanese life. The role of the Emperor changed radically. A
new constitution replaced the old one. These changes and

---

* Throughout these books I shall follow the Japanese practice of put-
ting family name first and given name second.

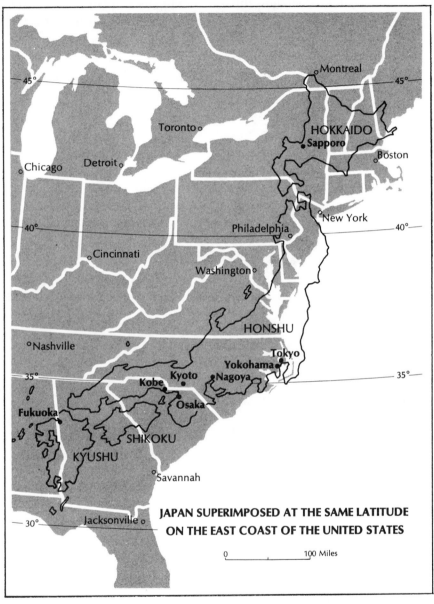

Montreal

45°   45°

Toronto○   HOKKAIDO
                              ●Sapporo
                                              ○Boston
○Chicago   Detroit○

                                              ○New York

40°   Philadelphia   40°
    ○Cincinnati   ○

        Washington○

                    HONSHU

○Nashville   ○   ●Tokyo
                        Yokohama●
35°   Kobe Kyoto ●Nagoya   35°
    ○   ●   ●
Fukuoka●   ●Osaka

        SHIKOKU
    KYUSHU

        ○Savannah

                JAPAN SUPERIMPOSED AT THE SAME LATITUDE
30°   Jacksonville○ ON THE EAST COAST OF THE UNITED STATES

                    0   100 Miles

(From E. O. Reischauer, Japan: The Story of a Nation, *New York: Alfred A. Knopf, 1970)*

others left a deep imprint on the Japanese people. How do they view the past? What does being Japanese mean to them?

This book examines some of these contemporary social issues. It also attempts to set these issues in historical context, indicating the unique route Japan has traveled to get where it is today.

The Affluent Society

⪦§ Editor's Introduction: Japan today is one of the world's economic giants. It ranks third today in gross national product, behind the United States and the Soviet Union.

This economic performance has resulted in a middle-class life for a high percentage of Japan's population. The following reading describes the life of a salaried worker, the hypothetical Watanabe Masao.

How different is his life from the lives of American white-collar workers? §⪧

Watanabe Masao: 40, married, two children (daughter, 11, son, 9), deputy chief of a department division in a large trading company, annual salary $18,000.

Like almost 90 per cent of all Japanese, Watanabe Masao believes himself firmly ensconced in middle class life. And the great majority of these people believe themselves to represent "middle-middle class' living.

Life styles in Japan have become widely standardized due to the extreme breadth of this middle class existence. There are a surprisingly small number of very rich or very poor families in today's Japan; and middle class families throughout the nation have come to accept certain standards of life as normal for their situation, due in large part to the almost total saturation rates for newspapers and televisions.

The Mega-Class

Throughout the entire range of self-styled middle class families there are definite variances in income; but the tastes and aspirations of this "mega-class" tend to become more and more similar, based on idealized images of what middle class life should resemble.

Our middle class "everyman", Watanabe Masao, is drawn

As this view of Tokyo indicates, affluence in our world involves the automobile. Although many of these headlights represent taxis, many also represent private cars. (Consulate General of Japan, N.Y.)

to fit this image of the middle class standard, and to give an idea of just what life style the average Japanese anticipates.

Although active in sports during his youth, Watanabe is now a little bothered by middle-age spread because of the sedentary nature of his work. He also has begun counting the grey hairs, but scoffs at the thought of dyeing it (" . . . but maybe if I did it gradually . . . ").

Home Owner

Two years ago, Watanabe moved his family to a newly-purchased house in the suburbs of Tokyo. Although the home is small, it affords a welcome sense of security unknown during the past two decades of apartment-dwelling. But after alloting space to park his compact car, Watanabe discovered that his garden area was just about big enough for a few flowers and two trees.

Leaving home at 7:30 each morning, Watanabe takes a short bus ride to the nearby railway station, then stands on a crowded train for almost an hour before arriving at his downtown stop. "No chance to get a seat," he comments, "unless we had moved all the way to the end of the line." Just a few stops before his destination, Watanabe spots a fellow worker squeezing his way into the now-jampacked commuter train. "Morning, Tanaka. Just two more wins and the Giants will take the Central League pennant again this year." "Right," answers the younger man. "And I'm going to the doubleheader Sunday to watch them clinch it."

After a discussion of the pro baseball season now coming to a close, and the odds on which team will take the championship, Watanabe and Tanaka walk through an underground passage from the station, entering directly into their office building. "By the way, Tanaka, when are you going to get married? I'd have thought some smart girl would have snapped up a promising young businessman like you long ago." "Not me," says Watanabe's friend. "I like living downtown in an apartment. I couldn't stand that hour-long sardine can ride of yours every morning." "Don't let that stop you," Watanabe says, "because with the price of land these days you might be retired before you can afford your own home."

(Land and housing prices are among the biggest worries of the middle class. Less than half of the urban workers now own their own homes.)

Work Environment

Arriving at his desk, Watanabe is greeted by his staff who immediately check the day's schedule with him. He gulps a quick cup of tea made by one of the office workers and then turns to answer the phone which starts ringing promptly at 9 to begin the workday.

At noon, Watanabe and his boss lunch together in the company restaurant. Afterwards they stop at a coffee shop before going back to work. Their conversation centers at first around world economic conditions, then finally settles on more immediate business concerns. They worry about inflation and food prices, the slowed pace of their company's business since the oil crisis of 1973, and, of course, prospects for promotion in the company.

Both men are of the generation which accepted the idea that "work and family" were the things that made life worthwhile, and neither finds it easy to accept change of pace resulting from the business slowdown of recent years and the growing trend toward increased leisure time. They became used to working overtime, six days a week and even sometimes on Sundays during their early days with the company; and the recent adoption of a five-day work week has left them feeling a bit uncomfortable. Watanabe and his boss have a firm concept of achievement. They hope to climb the established ladder from deputy division chief to full chief, to assistant and then full department head, to bureau director and finally to the upper rungs of the executive level.

That executive level, the doorway to "upper class" life, is their eventual goal, and their ambition is based more on providing a good future for their children than enjoying personal pleasures.

After work, Watanabe stops at a bar or cocktail lounge for a few drinks with his associates (once or twice a month he entertains company clients on an expense account). He may play mahjong one or two nights a week, and rarely arrives home before 8-9 p.m. On Saturday morning he'll meet his friends for their regular twice-monthly round of golf, and on Sunday he'll take his wife and son for a drive in the country. But that may be the last Sunday drive for son Jiro for quite a long time, for from the following week the boy will begin attending a *juku* (a private school where supplementary study is provided to help school children get good grades as well as pass examinations to higher schools). Watanabe's daughter has already been going to a *juku* for several years, for the doting father is intense in his desire to see his children move up the educational ladder without having to suffer the so-called examination "hell", as the extremely competitive examinations for admission to the university, or even high school, are called.

Watanabe Masao is an average, middle class, white-collar office worker. His life rotates around his job and family; and most of his activity is devoted to improving the chances for his children's future. He can be seen by the hundreds of thousands every morning at the railway stations and office buildings of Tokyo, Osaka and other cities.

JAPANESE TOURISTS, 1979

During the calendar year 1979, more than 4,000,000 Japanese traveled to other countries. This figure represents an increase of 800% over the number 10 years earlier.

Roughly 1,300,000 tourists travelled to the United States, 600,000 to Taiwan, 500,000 to South Korea, and 200,000 to the Philippines.

Japan Report, May 1, 1980

Big Boss of
the Thunder Herd

≈§Editor's Introduction: Miss Suzuki and the other workers mentioned in the last selection are just beginning to reap the benefits of affluence. Their role in Japan's economic boom has been central, for industry cannot get far without armies of willing workers.

But there must also be vision at the top.

Here is a description of the man behind the success of the Honda Motor Company. What are his values and goals? How do you think he would fare in the American business world?§≈

"I THINK BEST when I have a wrench in my hands," says Honda Soichiro, head of Honda Motor Co. Ltd., which has made motorcyclists out of over nine million people throughout the world and will soon invade the United States with a snappy midget sedan and a racy sports car. Honda has an awesome office overlooking Tokyo, as befits the boss of a $330 million empire, but he has been there only twice in the past two years and rarely attends his own monthly directors' meetings. Instead, the man Japanese call "Big Boss of the Thunder Herd" enmeshes himself in the grease and clatter of his research lab, dressed in white overalls and green-and-white baseball cap. He

Maynard Parker, *Life* Magazine © 1967 Time Inc. Reprinted with permission.

Honda Soichiro goes over design plans in his research lab. (American Honda Motor Co., Inc.)

runs eagerly about, fiddling with carburetors, stopping for a bowl of noodles in the workers' cafeteria, his playful face often exploding with laughter. Instead of bowing and calling him "Honorable President," the workers call him "Pop." But when his famous temper explodes they call him the *kaminari* (thunderbolt). He seems blissfully oblivious to such things as sales and marketing. "If you make a superior product," he says, "people will buy it."

Honda Soichiro, who is 60, was 8 when he saw his first motorcar. It was a Model T Ford, one of the first cars to come to Japan, and it clattered its way through the small town of Hamamatsu, 120 miles south of Tokyo, where Honda's father was the village blacksmith. Honda ran excitedly after the car. "It leaked oil," he recalls, "and I got down on my hands and knees to smell it. It was like perfume."

It was the beginning of a love affair. In school, Honda would sit in the back of the room, whittling wooden blocks into things that looked like engines. His favorite toy was a pair of his father's pliers, which he had taken to bed with him ever since he was a small boy. When he was 18, he moved to Tokyo to become an apprentice at an auto repair shop, but to prove himself worthy he had to spend six months babysitting for the boss's three children.

When he was 22, he opened his own repair shop. In his spare time, he built racers: one vehicle powered by a converted airplane engine roared along at 70 mph. He next souped up an old Ford and set a new all-Japan record of 75 mph before cracking up the machine in a spectacular crash that tossed him 15 feet into the air and broke his arm and shoulder.

During the war he manufactured piston rings and propellers for Zero fighters, but Allied bombing soon reduced his small shop to ruins. After the war, which left Japan almost bereft of motorized vehicles, Honda foresaw a great need for cheap transportation. In 1948, he scrounged 500 engines discarded by the Imperial Army, attached them to bicycles, and began turning out motorbikes. Since gas was then severely rationed, he fueled them with an extract made from crushed pine roots. Despite the fact that the first models took 20 minutes of pumping to get them started, the bikes sold quickly. He improved the engines, and in five years sales reached $6.7 million. But, says Honda, "I wanted to be Number One in the world, not just in Japan."

To overcome prewar Japan's reputation for shoddy, bamboo-and-beer-can merchandise, Honda entered his cycles in Europe's Grand Prix races. European racers scoffed: "We didn't think the Japanese made anything except rickshaws," said one. The first year, Honda's entries ran dead last.

For weeks, Honda followed the racing circuit about Europe, spending days and nights redesigning and rebuilding. The work paid off. Within two years, Honda's cycles swept seven of the top ten races, amazing European manufacturers. "It's time the British firms copied Japanese know-how," blustered the London *Daily Mirror*. One British expert took one of Honda's bikes apart piece by piece, then exclaimed in awe, "The bloody thing is made like a watch.". . .

Besides motorcycles and cars, Honda has pushed his company into making farm machinery, lawn mowers, generators, and a variety of industrial engines. But he has avoided the wide-ranging diversification of many Japanese firms. "If it doesn't have a motor," he says, "I don't want to build it."

Quotations from Mr. Honda

"When I drive, I almost feel like a god. It is always difficult for me to comprehend that half the world is not yet even in the bicycle stage and most of the other half is just entering the motorcycle stage."

"My biggest thrill is when I plan something and it fails. My mind is then filled with ideas on how I can improve it. There is nothing for me in my life but my work. I think so much about it I sometimes have to take a sleeping pill if I have something important to do the next day so I can be well rested."

"I don't require my engineers to have diplomas. When I was going to school before the war, the principal told me I had failed because even though I was Number One in the class, I hadn't taken the final. I told him, 'I don't give a damn for the diploma. What I want is the knowledge.'"

Editor's Postscript: In many ways Honda is typical of Japan's top business executives. Most of them are hard workers, dedicated to the success of their enterprise. Says Takenaka Renichi, president of Japan's largest construction company, "Japanese corporate executives are really very simple men who live simple lives and have one simple aim: We want our companies and hopefully our country to be the very best possible. We leave the 'high life' to other people—and other places."

The simple life is characteristic of these tycoons. Says Yoshiyama Hirokichi, president of a top company manufacturing electrical equipment, "It is not the Japanese way to flaunt one's wealth. My wife and I live in a five-room apartment here in Tokyo and it is quite sufficient for us. In my opinion, luxuries only complicate life."

NISSAN AND HONDA
BUILD IN THE U.S.

Nissan Motor Company has become the second Japanese automaker to build an assembly plant in the United States. In early 1980 Honda Motor Company decided to build an assembly plant in Ohio. The Nissan plant, to be located either in the Great Lakes region or in the Southeast, will produce 10,000 pick-up trucks per month.

Japan's Economy

Gross National Product. A country's gross national product (GNP) is the sum total of the goods and services produced in a given year. Japan's GNP in 1977 was more than $600 billion, the third highest in the world. Japan trails only the United States (1977 GNP $1,900 billion) and the Soviet Union (1977 GNP estimated at $1,000 billion.)

But Japan's growth has not been uniform throughout the economy. Over-all industrial production has increased since 1950 many times over. However, mine production has changed little in the same period. Today's rice crop is less than that of 1960. Wheat and barley production is 1/6 that of 1960 (98% of Japan's wheat and barley is imported).

It is manufacturing which has led the way. The increase in

By Richard H. Minear. Please see the Teacher's Guide for data which brings the charts on pp. 26, 27, 29 and 31 up to date as of 1978.

GROWTH IN PRODUCTION OF SELECTED MANUFACTURES

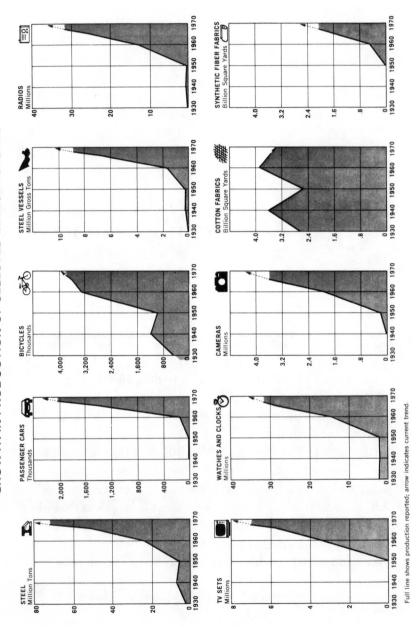

Full line shows production reported; arrow indicates current trend.

(From Geography in an Urban Age, Unit 6, Japan, New York: Macmillan, 1966, p. 65)

the production of manufactures since 1960 is about 500%. A consideration of selected products yields a striking picture. In which fields has growth been most dramatic?

Energy. Japan's industrial boom in the years after World War II has increased the demand for energy. Japan relies now on three major types of energy: hydroelectric power, thermal power, and atomic power. Hydroelectric power comes from dams; thermal power comes from steam-driven turbines. The turbines require fuel, mainly coal and oil—and Japan is virtually lacking in these natural resources. Hence Japan's

ELECTRIC POWER GENERATED

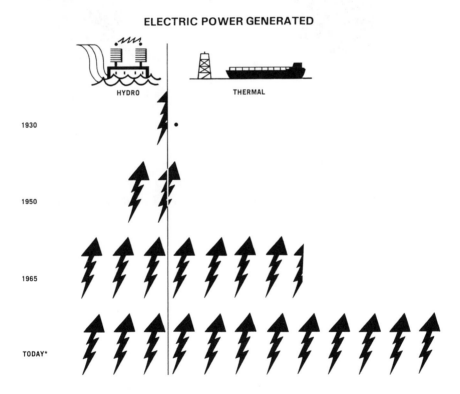

HYDRO   THERMAL

1930

1950

1965

TODAY*

Each complete symbol represents 25 billion kilowatt hours.
● Negligible.   *TODAY is estimated output for 1970.

(*From* Geography in an Urban Age, *Unit 6,* Japan, *New York: Macmillan, 1966, p. 103*)

28

DIRECTION OF JAPAN'S FOREIGN TRADE

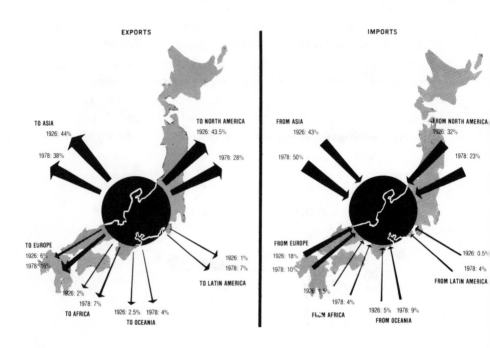

(Updated from *Geography in an Urban Age, Unit 6, Japan,* New York: MacMillan, 1966, p.108)

vulnerability to changes in the price and availability of imported oil, far more than the United States. This also explains the rapid increase in Japan's atomic power capability since 1970.

― *Foreign Trade.* The industrial products that have highlighted Japan's economic growth are highly exportable. This is not accidental. Because Japan must import fuel and other natural resources, she must export goods to pay for these imports. Still, Japan herself consumes the lion's share of her own industrial production.

In 1978 Japan *imported* goods valued at $75 billion.

DEMAND AND SUPPLY FOR SELECTED PRODUCTS

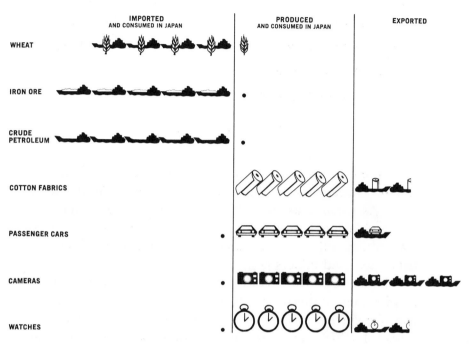

Each symbol represents 20 per cent of quantity consumed in Japan in 1967.
● Less than 2.5 per cent of quantity consumed in Japan.

(*From* Geography in an Urban Age, *Unit 6,* Japan, *New York: Macmillan, 1966, p. 107*)

Important imports included the following:

foodstuffs	$2.4 billion
light industry products	6.3 billion
raw materials and fuels	9.9 billion
heavy industry products	10.3 billion

In the same year Japan *exported* goods valued at $92.5 billion. Important exports included:

foodstuffs	$1.0 billion
raw materials and fuels	.8 billion
light industry products	10.6 billion
heavy industry products	79.3 billion *

* Passenger cars accounted for $10.1 billion of this figure.

Labor Force. The industrial boom has transformed Japan's employment picture, as the chart on page 31 makes clear. As recently as 1940, 45 percent of the work force was engaged in agriculture, fishing, and mining. In 1978 the figure was about 11%. Where have the disappearing farmers, fishermen, and miners gone?

Japanese education has kept pace with the changes in the employment pattern. In 1925 75% of the labor force had completed elementary school and only 5% had completed high school. In 1978 there were 10.7 million Japanese between the ages of 20 and 24. Of these, 58% had completed high school (another 30% had completed junior high); 6% had graduated from junior colleges; and 4% had graduated from a four-year college or university.

Japan and the Energy Crisis. More than any other major nation, Japan is vulnerable to the energy crisis. As the second largest energy-consuming nation in the non-Communist world, Japan uses oil "like an alcoholic going through a quart of scotch." Moreover, Japan must import 85 percent of its energy needs, including 99.8 percent of its oil. In 1978 54% of this oil came from two oil-exporting countries: Saudi Arabia (36%) and Iran (18%). Japan's oil bill in 1978 was well over $20 billion.

To pay this staggering bill, Japan must increase its exports. The chart on page 29, updated to 1978, demonstrates how the exports of passenger cars has grown. In 1965 Japan exported only 200,000 vehicles (cars *and* trucks); in 1978, it exported

EMPLOYED PERSONS, BY INDUSTRY

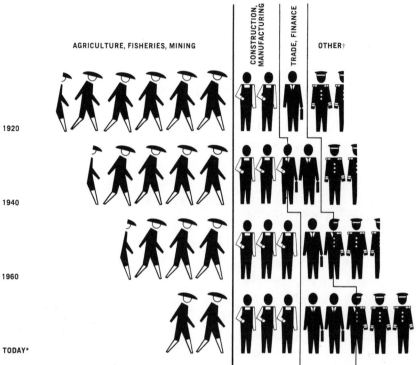

Each complete symbol represents 10 per cent of the employed population.
†OTHER includes transportation, communication, services, and government.
*TODAY is estimate for 1970.

(*From* Geography in an Urban Age, *Unit 6,* Japan, *New York: Mac-millan, 1966, p. 64*)

2,800,000 passenger cars alone. In 1980 Japan exported an estimated 1,820,000 passenger cars to the United States.

However, expanding Japanese exports create problems for the economies of the countries which receive these exports. Witness the cries of the American auto industry in 1981 for protection against Japanese imports. But if the Japanese auto industry is markedly more efficient than Detroit, protection serves primarily to protect inefficient producers.

At the end of April 1981 the Japanese government yielded to American demands and agreed to restrict exports of passenger cars to 1,680,000 in the following 12 months. Writing soon thereafter, one American commentator argued that the restrictions are "a giant charade." They have "little to do with the (American auto) industry's recovery" but "very much to do with its politics. They are the one thing that (American) companies and unions can agree upon." And in Washington calling for restrictions "spares politicians the distasteful task of talking about past management mistakes and excess labor costs."

In any case, restrictions are disturbingly reminiscent of the narrow economic nationalism which constituted one cause of Japanese-American antagonism in the 1930s. Today the major economies of the world are closely interlocked. Major disruptions in Japan have an enormous impact in the United States, and vice versa.

Japan Today

The Quality of Life

◂§Editor's Introduction: The quality of life in Japan today is no easier to describe than the quality of life in America. But one way to get a sense of how contemporary Japan appears to the Japanese is to read Japanese literature.

The following selection is an excerpt from a Japanese novel first published in 1964. The main character is a man known simply as Bird. As the novel opens, Bird's wife is in the hospital giving birth to their first child. The birth is difficult and prolonged, and Bird has fled the hospital and is roaming the streets of the city.

What is there about Bird and his environment—if anything— that seems to you peculiarly Japanese?§▸

BIRD EMERGED IN the square at the back of the honkytonk district, where the clamor and motion seemed to focus. The clock of lightbulbs on the theater in the center of the square was flashing SEVEN PM—time to ask about his wife. Bird had been telephoning his mother-in-law at the hospital every hour since three that afternoon. He glanced around the square. Plenty of public telephones, but all were occupied. . . .

Oe Kenzaburo, *A Personal Matter,* translated by John Nathan, pp. 8–14. Reprinted by permission of Grove Press, Inc. © 1968 by Grove Press, Inc.

Bird retraced his steps, glancing into bars and coffee
houses, Chinese noodle shops, cutlet restaurants, and shoe-
stores. He could always step inside somewhere and phone. But
he wanted to avoid a bar if he could, and he had eaten dinner
already. Why not buy a powder to settle his stomach?

Bird was looking for a drugstore when an outlandish establishment on a corner stopped him short. On a giant bill-
board suspended above the door a cowboy crouched with a

*Young Japanese who don't like the Big Mac may prefer Dunkin
Donuts or Kentucky Fried Chicken. All three chains have begun
operation in Japan.* (Copyright by Doug Hurst)

pistol flaming. Bird read the legend that flowered on the head of the Indian pinned beneath the cowboy's spurs: GUN CORNER. Inside, beneath paper flags of the United Nations and strips of spiraling green and yellow crepe paper, a crowd much younger than Bird was milling around the many-colored, box-shaped games that filled the store from front to back. Bird, ascertaining through the glass doors rimmed with red and indigo tape that a public telephone was installed in a corner at the rear, stepped into the Gun Corner, passed a Coke machine and a juke box howling rock-n-roll already out of vogue, and started across the muddy wooden floor. It was instantly as if skyrockets were bursting in his ears. Bird toiled across the room as though he were walking in a maze, past pinball machines, dart games, and a miniature forest alive with deer and rabbits and monstrous green toads that moved on a conveyer belt; as Bird passed, a high-school boy bagged a frog under the admiring eyes of his girlfriends, and five points clicked into the window on the side of the game. He finally reached the telephone. . . .

The phone rang four times before his mother-in-law's voice, like his wife's made somewhat younger, answered; Bird immediately asked about his wife. . . .

"Nothing yet. It just won't come; that child is suffering to death and the baby just won't come!"

Wordless, Bird stared for an instant at the numberless antholes in the ebonite receiver. The surface, like a night sky vaulted with black stars, clouded and cleared with each breath he took.

"I'll call back at eight," he said a minute later, then hung up the phone, and sighed.

A drive-a-car game was installed beside the phone, and a boy who looked like a Filipino was seated behind the wheel. . . . On and on he drove, biting his thin lips shut with keen eyeteeth and spraying the air with sibilant saliva, as if convinced that finally the belt would cease to revolve and bring the E-type Jaguar to its destination. But the road unfurled obstacles in front of the little car unendingly. Now and then, when the belt began to slow down, the Filipino would plunge a hand

Every Japanese city has hundreds of pinball parlors. This young laborer has dropped in for a half-hour of play. (Copyright by Doug Hurst)

into his pants pocket, grope out a coin, and insert it in the metal eye of the machine. Bird paused where he stood obliquely behind the boy, and watched the game for a while. Soon a sensation of unbearable fatigue crept into his feet. Bird hurried toward the back exit, stepping as though the floor were scorching metal plate. At the back of the gallery, he encountered a pair of truly bizarre machines.

The game on the right was surrounded by a gang of youngsters in identical silk jackets embroidered with gold-and-silver brocade dragons, the Hong Kong souvenir variety designed for American tourists. They were producing loud, unfamiliar noises that sounded like heavy impacts. Bird approached the game on the left, because for the moment it was unguarded. It was a medieval instrument of torture, an Iron Maiden—twentieth-century model. A beautiful, life-sized

maiden of steel with mechanical red-and-black stripes was pro-
tecting her bare chest with stoutly crossed arms. The player
attempted to pull her arms away from her chest for a glimpse
of her hidden metal breasts; his grip and pull appeared as
numbers in the windows which were the maiden's eyes. Above
her head was a chronological table of average grip and pull.

Bird inserted a coin in the slot between the maiden's lips.
Then he set about forcing her arms way from her breasts. The
steel arms resisted stubbornly: Bird pulled harder. Gradually
his face was drawn in to her iron chest. Since her face was
painted in what was unmistakably an expression of anguish,
Bird had the feeling that he was raping the girl. He strained
until every muscle in his body began to ache. Suddenly there
was a rumbling in her chest as a gear turned, and numbered
plaques, the color of watery blood, clicked into her hollow
eyes. Bird went limp, panting, and checked his score against
the table of averages. It was unclear what the units repre-
sented, but Bird had scored 70 points for grip and 75 points
for pull. In the column on the table beneath 27 [his age], Bird
found GRIP: 110—PULL: 110. He scanned the table in disbelief
and discovered that his score was average for a man of forty.
Forty!—the shock dropped straight to his stomach and he
brought up a belch. Twenty-seven years and four months old
and no more grip nor pull than a man of forty: Bird! But how
could it be? On top of everything, he could tell that the
tingling in his shoulders and sides would develop into an ob-
stinate muscle ache. Determined to redeem his honor, Bird
approached the game on the right. He realized with surprise
that he was now in deadly earnest about this game of testing
strength.

With the alertness of wild animals whose territory is being invaded, the boys in dragon jackets froze as Bird moved in
and enveloped him with challenging looks. Rattled, but with a
fair semblance of carelessness, Bird inspected the machine at
the center of their circle. In construction it resembled a gallows
in a Western movie, except that a kind of Slavic cavalry helmet was suspended from the spot where a hapless outlaw

should have hung. The helmet only partly concealed a sand-bag covered in black buckskin. When a coin was inserted in the hole that glared like a cyclops's eye from the center of the helmet, the player could lower the sandbag and the indicator needle reset itself at zero. There was a cartoon of Robot Mouse in the center of the indicator: he was screaming, his yellow mouth open wide, *C'mon Killer; Let's Measure Your Punch!*

When Bird merely eyed the game and made no move in its direction, one of the dragon-jackets stepped forward as if to demonstrate, dropped a coin into the helmet, and pulled the sandbag down. Self-consciously but confident, the youth dropped back a step and, hurling his entire body forward as in a dance, walloped the sandbag. A heavy thud: the rattle of the chain as it crashed against the inside of the helmet. The needle leaped past the numbers on the gauge and quivered meaning-lessly. The gang exploded in laughter. The punch had ex-ceeded the capacity of the gauge: the paralyzed mechanism would not reset. The triumphant dragon-jacket aimed a light kick at the sandbag, this time from a karate crouch, and the indicator needle dropped to 500 while the sandbag crawled back into the helmet slowly like an exhausted hermit crab. Again the gang roared.

An unaccountable passion seized Bird. . . . He took off his jacket and laid it on a bingo table. Then he dropped into the helmet one of the coins from a pocketful he was carrying for phone calls to the hospital. The boys were watching every move. Bird lowered the sandbag, took one step back, and put up his fists. After he had been expelled from high school, in the days when he was studying for the examination that had qualified him to go to college, Bird had brawled almost every week with other delinquents in his provincial city. He had been feared, and he had been surrounded always by younger admirers. Bird had faith in the power of his punch. And his form would be orthodox, he wouldn't take that kind of un-gainly leap. Bird shifted his weight to the balls of his feet, took one light step forward, and smashed the sandbag with a right jab. Had his punch surpassed the limit of 2500 and made a cripple of the gauge? Like hell it had—the needle stood at 300! Doubled over, with his punching fist against his chest, Bird stared for an instant at the gauge in stupefaction. Then hot blood climbed into his face. Behind him the boys in dragon jackets were silent and still. But certainly their attention was concentrated on Bird and on the gauge; the appearance of a man with a punch so numerically meager must have struck them dumb.

Bird, moving as though unaware the gang existed, returned to the helmet, inserted another coin, and pulled the sandbag down. This was no time to worry about correct form: he threw the weight of his entire body behind the punch. His right arm went numb from the elbow to the wrist and the needle stood at a mere 500.

Stooping quickly, Bird picked up his jacket and put it on, facing the bingo table. Then he turned back to the teenagers, who were observing him in silence. Bird tried for an experienced smile, full of understanding and surprise, for the young champ from the former champion long retired. But the boys merely stared at him with blank, hardened faces, as though they were watching a dog. Bird turned crimson all the way behind his ears, hung his head, and hurried out of the gallery. A great guffawing erupted behind him, full of obviously affected glee.

Editor's Postscript: The term "culture shock" has been used to describe what happens when a person confronts a culture that is strange to him, perhaps when on a trip or in the Peace Corps. The social conventions with which he is familiar do not govern the new situation, and it takes time to learn new rules.

But is "culture shock" an accurate description of what Americans experience in Japan today? Some years ago an anthropologist from New York with experience in many areas of East Asia had this to say:

> I live in New York City. My friends here all talk about these three things: pollution, the cost of living, and how to find a parking space. I go to Tokyo, or to Taipei [in Taiwan], or to Bangkok [in Thailand]. My friends there all talk about three things: pollution,

the cost of living, and parking. Culture shock? Ridiculous! But when I go to small-town America, *then* I undergo culture shock.

What do you think? Is the New Yorker closer to the Tokyo resident than he is to the John Does of rural America? Is the Tokyo resident closer to the Chicagoan than he is to the Tanaka Taros of rural Japan?

What do the American big-city dweller and the Tokyoite have in common? What separates them?&

JAPANESE WIN
MUSIC COMPETITIONS

Three Japanese violinists placed first, third, and fourth in the 29th Queen Elizabeth International Competition held in Brussels. The winner, Horigome Yuzuko, a 23-year-old woman, graduated this year from Toho University. . . . A Japanese flutist has also won the Jean Pierre Rampal International Competition held in Paris this year. [He is] Kodo Shigenari, a 26-year-old man, graduated from the Conservatoire International Superieur de Musique de Paris with outstanding grades in 1978.

Japan Report, July 1980

A Closed Society: 1600-1853

≈§Editor's Introduction: Japan today is a cosmopolitan nation. It is one of the economic and technological giants of the world. It is deeply involved in international trade. Indeed, Japan depends on trade for its economic success.

But only 120 years ago Japan was a very different place. Its economy was largely agricultural. Its technology was "backward." Its foreign trade was almost nonexistent. For all practical purposes, Japan was cut off from the rest of the world.

The geography of Asia—the fact that Japan is separated from the mainland by 120 miles of water—made isolation possible, but it was a decision of the Japanese government that made isolation a reality.

From 1600 to 1868, Japan deliberately and systematically avoided contact with other people. Here are five articles from an exclusion edict issued by the Japanese government in 1636:

1. No Japanese ships may leave for foreign countries.
2. No Japanese may go abroad secretly. If anyone tries to do this, he will be killed, and the ship and owner(s) will be placed under arrest while higher authority is informed.
3. Any Japanese now living abroad who tries to return to Japan will be put to death.
4. No offspring of Southern Barbarians [Europeans] will be allowed to remain. Anyone violating this order will be killed and all his relatives punished according to the gravity of the offense.
5. If any deportees should try to return or to communicate with Japan by letter or otherwise, they will of course be killed if they are caught.

By Richard H. Minear.

At this time, only a very few Dutch, Chinese, and Korean traders were allowed into Japan. All others learned to stay away. If they didn't, they paid a high price.

In 1640 a Portuguese expedition—one ship with 74 men—sought to reopen trade with Japan. The Japanese authorities arrested the men and executed 61 of them. The remaining 13 were spared so that they could carry the word back to the outside world. At the burial ground, where the heads of the executed sailors were displayed on wooden poles, the Japanese authorities erected a sign with this message:

> A similar penalty will be suffered by all those who henceforward come to these shores from Portugal, whether they be ambassadors or whether they be sailors, whether they come by error or whether they be driven hither by storm. Even more, if the King of Portugal, or Buddha, or even the God of the Christians were to come, they would all pay the very same penalty.

Why did the Japanese pursue this policy of exclusion? What kind of society would want to isolate itself from the rest of the world? There are no easy answers to these questions, but the following selection, based on the recollections of a number of Japanese born and brought up in the early nineteenth century, supplies some insight into the nature of Japanese society during the long period of isolation.༄

SUZUKI TARO WAS born in 1832 in a town 150 miles west of present-day Tokyo (then called Edo). By then, the government of the *shogun,* or military governor based in Tokyo, had been in power for more than 200 years. It was shogunal policy to minimize change, to freeze Japanese society into a rigid social-class structure. For this reason, little in Japan in 1832 was unpredictable. In 1832 any of Taro's fellow Japanese, knowing a few basic facts about Taro's background, could have predicted just how he would be brought up and just how he would spend his life.

Taro was born a samurai, a warrior. His father had been a samurai. His sons would be samurai. It was far better to be born a samurai than to be born a farmer or a merchant. Only about one person in twenty was a samurai, and only samurai could bear swords or hold administrative office. The vast majority of the population, 80 per cent or more, were farmers.

The others were artisans and merchants, except for a tiny group of Buddhist and Shinto priests and monks and a tiny group of outcasts—people who did such unclean tasks as tanning hides.

Swords were part of Taro's life from a very early age. His parents were so happy their new child was a boy that they had trouble restraining themselves from giving him a sword almost at birth. But restrain themselves they did, and Taro had only wooden swords to play with until he was five. It was indeed a time for celebration when Taro's father presented him with his first real sword. Taro continued often to wear a wooden sword instead of the real thing, but he had taken a major step on the road to samurai manhood. Outside his home, he was never

The castle of Taro's lord was not so grand as this one, the house of one of the most important lords of northern Japan. (Japan National Tourist Organization)

without a sword, real or wooden, and people who saw him on
the street knew immediately that he was a samurai.

From the age of fifteen on, Taro carried two swords: a
long sword and a short one. To carry these instruments of death
at all times made Taro deeply aware of his mission in life, the
mission of all samurai: to serve his lord bravely and loyally,
and to set an example for others. Should any situation arise in
which dishonor seemed likely, Taro would use the short sword
to end his own life, displaying in his ritual suicide his selfless-
ness and devotion to his lord.

To grow up as a samurai meant learning the military arts,
so Taro spent many hours wrestling and fencing and riding and
studying archery. But Japan had enjoyed nearly two hundred
years of peace, and in peacetime one needed other skills as
well. So Taro studied reading and writing and, as he grew
older, began to read the Chinese classics.

Taro's training was strict, for becoming a worthy samurai
was not an easy task. At the age of six Taro began to memorize
the Chinese classics. At the time, the words meant very little
to him, and he memorized only the sounds. But his teachers
were sure that gradually the wisdom of the sages would penetrate his young mind, that what he had at first merely memorized would eventually take on real meaning. To his dying day,
Taro was able to recite long passages from the classics.

Taro met his teacher all during the year. Fall and spring
were no problem, but the heat of the summer sometimes made
him so weak he thought he would faint. The winter cold
brought a different kind of suffering. His clothing was not
heavy, and the room was unheated. Using a fire simply to
warm himself Taro knew was the way of a weakling. When
his hands became too cold to hold his writing brush, his teacher
would say, "Dip them in that bucket of water." The water in
the bucket was ice-cold. When his bare feet became numb,
his teacher would say, "Go run around in the snow."

There were many things Taro was not allowed to do
simply because he was a samurai. For instance, at home he
never saw a *samisen,* perhaps the most important musical

instrument of his day. Why not? Because the music of the
samisen was unworthy for samurai to hear. Townsmen, maybe,
but not samurai. For the same reason, Taro never saw a *kabuki*
play. When the *kabuki* players came around, Taro's lord
would issue orders reminding the samurai not to attend. The
temptation was strong, for *kabuki* offered songs and dances
and fine actors and exciting plots, and more than once Taro
wished he could see what went on inside the theater.

Samurai were supposed to be above such matters as money
and commerce. Ideally, a samurai never handled money. But
Taro, like most samurai, had no servants, and so he often wound
up going to the market himself. To hide his embarrassment,
he usually went out after dark.

Taro's family and almost all the other samurai families
lived near the castle of the lord. The castle sat high on a hill,
with a moat, thick walls, and a tall tower. The lord himself
and his two most trusted advisers lived in the castle. The rest
of the samurai lived in the houses spread out around the lower
slopes of the hill. The most important samurai families lived
closest to the castle walls. Taro's family was not very important
(Taro's father could never become a high official or have a
personal interview with the lord) and therefore lived down the
hill, closer to the temples and stores of the town.

A few temples and a moat separated Taro's neighborhood from the quarter set aside for the townsmen—artisans and
merchants. No artisan or merchant could live near Taro, nor
was Taro permitted to live in their quarter.

Even though townsmen and samurai lived within a stone's
throw of each other, their lives were worlds apart. A townsman
of Taro's age could not go to the official school. He could not
wear a sword or fine clothes. He could not ride in that day's
version of a taxi—a small compartment suspended from a
pole carried on the shoulders of two bearers. Townsmen could
not build three-story buildings or use gold and silver leaf in
decorating their houses. Taro's house occupied a fair-sized lot
with a broad front on the street; but the houses of townsmen
were built on smaller lots, with only narrow fronts.

Samurai ride again—this time in one of Japan's many historical pageants. (Japan National Tourist Organization)

As a samurai, Taro was free to walk through the townsmen's quarter, and he did so often: past the street of the armorers, closest to the samurai quarter, and then past the street of the rice dealers, the fish market, and the street of the *tatami* makers. But townsmen were not so free to wander. They had to stay out of the samurai quarter except when they had a specific reason for entering. Still, the regulations were not so strict in Taro's town as in some other towns, where townsmen were required to remove their wooden clogs before entering the samurai district.

As Taro walked on past the *tatami* makers, he came to a border area between town and country. Here he saw temples and shrines and cemeteries, along with an irrigation ditch, which could serve as a first line of defense. Beyond the border area lay the countryside, a checkerboard of small rice paddies with a tiny farm village every mile or so.

On a fine June day, Taro would find the fields full of farmers—men, women, and children—knee-deep in mud, transplanting rice seedlings to be harvested in November. The stench was almost overpowering, for the farmers collected human excrement from the town to fertilize their fields. Taro thanked his stars that he was a samurai when he saw how these farmers labored. Bending from the waist to push the seedlings into the mud with their bare fingers, the rice planters, mainly women, sometimes sang for relief from their brutal drudgery.

Taro's father served his lord in the capacity of overseer of four farm villages, so Taro had heard considerable discussion at home of the farmers and their problems. In theory, the farmers were a prized class: after all, they produced the rice crop that fed Japan and supported the government of the samurai. But Taro knew that reality was something different. Taxes on the farmers were very high. And last year had been a bad crop year: heavy rains had come just before the harvest, and much of the crop had rotted in the fields.

Indeed, Taro remembered his father's anxiety during the winter, when one group of farmers had seemed on the point of lodging formal protest with the lord. In a year of bad crops, they wanted the tax rate lowered. Taro's father had met with them and assuaged their anger, and the formal protest had not been made. That was certainly a good thing for Taro's father, and perhaps also for the farmers.

Had the protest been made, Taro's father might well have lost his job, been disgraced, and perhaps been driven to commit suicide in atonement. The lord expected his officials to control all matters within their jurisdiction. The fact that a group of farmers took political action—whatever the merits of their case—was enough to indicate that the official in charge was not fulfilling his duty. The farmers leading the protest might have been executed or deported, even if the lord determined that their protest was justified, for such unauthorized political action was a challenge to the stability of the social order. Farmers, after all, were farmers. They grew rice, paid taxes, and obeyed the directions of their natural superiors. Samurai were samurai. Samurai ruled. There could be no mixing of the two functions.

Taro had never ventured more than five miles away from home. From the top of the hill near his house he could see the ocean, but he had never been in a boat. Nor was it likely that he would travel at all until he was eighteen or twenty. Then his lord might well order him to Edo to serve there as a guard. This would mean a trip of 150 miles on foot that would take Taro a good ten days.

Should he get to Edo, he would meet for the first time samurai from other parts of the land. He would begin to sense the immense size of this land called Japan. He might even— perhaps—begin to think first of his duty to Japan and only second of his duty to his lord. Only the future would tell.

JAPANESE FIRMS TO BUILD PERSIAN GULF AIRPORT

Two Japanese companies have jointly been awarded a multi-million dollar contract for construction of airport buildings in Abu Dhabi. The contract, worth approximately $94 million, is the second largest construction project Japanese firms have landed abroad. It is surpassed in value only by the $142 million Suez Canal expansion project that went to a Tokyo firm after intense international competition.

Japan Report, November 16, 1976

The Old Values

⪧§*Editor's Introduction:* The samurai class had its origin in warfare, but for 250 years there was peace in Japan. What was the peacetime role of the samurai class? Here is one answer, given by a high-ranking samurai of the seventeenth century:

From ancient times the people have been divided into four classes: samurai, farmer, artisan, and merchant. Each class has its own vocation. The farmers devote themselves to agriculture; the artisans promote industry; and the merchants are engaged in trade. All three of these classes contribute to the good of society.

What, then, is the use of the samurai class? Its only vocation is to preserve righteousness. The people of other classes deal with visible things, while the samurai deal with invisible, colorless, and intangible things.

Since visible and invisible things are so different from each other, some may think that the members of the samurai class are entirely unnecessary. But if there were no samurai, righteousness would disappear from human society, the sense of shame would be lost, and wrong and injustice would prevail. In that case, you would seldom find a faithful subject, a dutiful son, or a trustworthy friend; and such shameful acts as cheating and stealing would be daily occurrences. In short, in the absence of the samurai the whole country would be thrown into great confusion. This is the chief reason why they are placed above other people. It is also why other people are pleased to pay them great respect, in spite of the fact that the samurai appear to have no visible occupation.*

* Adapted from "Instructions of a Mito Prince to His Retainers." Translated by Ernest W. Clement, in *Transactions of the Asiatic Society of Japan,* 26 (1898), 135–36.

The samurai saw themselves as the protectors of public virtue, the guardians of traditional values. Today, many Japanese see a marked similarity between the samurai of long ago and the Japanese salaried man of today. Like the samurai, the salaried man is the ideal type of his society. Just as the samurai served his lord, the salaried man serves his company. The samurai had his sword; the salaried man has his briefcase.

We may never fully understand how Japan was able to transform itself into a highly industrialized society, but surely part of the explanation lies in the realm of values, in the attitudes toward self and society that the Japanese brought with them into the modern world.

The following selection attempts to examine these traditional values by presenting evidence about the life-styles of the two most important classes, samurai and farmer. What similarities, if any, do you find between these traditional values and the modern values of the industrialist Honda?&

Recollections of a Seventeenth-Century Samurai

WHEN I WAS about sixteen I had a tendency toward corpulence. I had noticed a lack of agility in other fleshy persons and thought a heavy man would not make a first-class samurai. So I tried every means to keep myself agile and lean. I slept with my girdle drawn tight and stopped eating rice. I took no wine and abstained from sexual intercourse for the next ten years. While on duty at Edo, there were no hills or fields at hand where I could hunt and climb, so I exercised with spear and sword. When I was on the night watch at my master's residence in Edo, I kept a wooden sword and a pair of straw sandals in my bamboo hamper, and with these I used to put myself through military drill in the darkened court after everyone was asleep. I also practiced running about over the roofs of the outbuildings far removed from the sleeping rooms. This I did so as to be able to handle myself nimbly if a fire should break out.

From W. T. de Bary, ed., *Sources of Japanese Tradition* (New York: Columbia University Press, 1958), pp. 387–88.

There were a few who noticed me at these exercises and they were reported to have said that I was probably possessed by a hobgoblin. This was before I was twenty years old. After that I hardened myself by going into the fields on hot summer days and shooting skylarks with a gun, since I did not own a falcon for hawking. In the winter months I often spent several days in the mountains, taking no night clothes or bed quilt with me and wearing only a lined jacket of cotton over a thin cotton shirt. My little hamper was almost filled by my ink-stand, paper, books, and two wadded silk kimonos. I stayed overnight in any house I came across in my rambles.

In this way I disciplined myself until I was 37 or 38 years old and avoided becoming fleshy. I was fully aware of my want of talent and believed I could never hope to be of any great service to my country, so I was all the more resolved to do my best as a common *samurai* [one who could not aspire to high office].

From Eighteenth-Century Handbooks for Samurai

Every morning make up your mind how to die. Every evening freshen your mind in the thought of death. And do this without ceasing. Thus your mind will be prepared. When your mind is set always on death, your way through life will always be straight and simple. . . .

When you realize how for generations your family has served the house of your lord; when you remember how those who have gone before you served that house, and how those who will come after you will serve it—then you will be moved to a deep sense of gratitude. For you, there should be no thought but of service to the one master who has a claim on your grateful heart. . . .

When you leave a festive place, depart while you still want to stay. When you feel you are satisfied and ready to

Rice technology has changed remarkably little in the past two hundred years, except that yields, which were high in Taro's day, have become even higher. Here, farm women transplant rice seedlings. (Japan National Tourist Organization)

leave, you have already had too much. Enough is too much.*

Being on guard over oneself when one is alone means that the self-control which we exercise over our conduct when we are within the observation and hearing of other people should . . . be kept up when there is nobody else looking on or within hearing of us. No matter whether other people are . . . able to see or hear us, each one should . . . be careful how he behaves. Bad actions are easily found out. . . . "An evil deed runs a thousand miles," as the proverb says. . . .†

---

* Tamotsu Iwado, " 'Hagakure Bushidō' or the Book of the Warrior," *Cultural Nippon,* 7:3 (1939), 38–39, 55, 45.
† J. Carey Hall, "Teijo's Family Instructions," *Transactions and Proceedings of the Japan Society of London,* 14 (1916), 153, 146.

From a Nineteenth-Century Handbook for Farmers

Wealth and poverty are not far apart; the disparity between the two is only slight. Whether one attains wealth or is reduced to poverty depends upon the degree of his preparedness. A poor man works today or during the current year to dispose of the task he should have done yesterday or during last year. Accordingly, he struggles all through his life to no avail.

On the other hand, a wealthy man works today or during the current year to prepare himself for the needs of tomorrow or next year, so that he is at ease and free and succeeds in whatever thing he undertakes. Many people who have no rice wine to drink or rice to eat today will borrow money or rice. This is the cause that drives them into poverty.

If you gather wood today to boil rice with tomorrow morning, or if you make rope tonight for tying fences the next day, then you can be at your ease. But the poor man wants to boil rice tonight with wood he may gather the next day, or tie fences today with rope he may make tomorrow. Consequently, struggle as he may, he will not succeed.

Therefore, I often say . . . that unpreparedness is the cause of poverty. . . .

It is not by accident that one becomes rich or poor. Wealth comes from adequate causes, as does poverty. It is wrong to think, as people generally do, that wealth finds its way to those who are wealthy. As a matter of fact, it goes to those who are thrifty and industrious.

Adapted from Tadatsu Ishiguro, ed., *Ninomiya Sontoku* (Tokyo: Kenkyusha, 1955), pp. 131–32, 146–47, 155–57.

Fuji-ichi the Tycoon

Editor's Introduction: After the samurai and the farmers, the third important class in traditional Japanese society was the townsmen—the artisans and merchants. In theory, the artisans were superior to the merchants because they actually produced goods, whereas the merchants only sold goods that others had produced. But in reality, the artisans and merchants fused into one class. In theory, farmers outranked townsmen, but in reality townsmen were often much better off.

What values did these townsmen hold? How do these values compare with those of the samurai and the farmers? The following short story, published first in 1688, describes the activities of a miserly merchant. It does not tell the whole story of the townsman's life, of course, but it provides insight into the commercial values of the times. What image did the townsmen have of themselves? How do you think Fuji-ichi would succeed in the modern business world?

Fuji-ichi was a clever man, and his substantial fortune was amassed in his own lifetime. But first and foremost he was a man who knew his own mind, and this was the basis of his success. In addition to carrying on his regular business, he kept a separate ledger, bound from odd scraps of paper, in which, as he sat all day in his shop, pen in hand, he entered a variety of chance information. As the clerks from the money

Ihara Saikaku, "The Eternal Storehouse of Japan," translated by G. W. Sargent, in Donald Keene, ed., *Anthology of Japanese Literature* (New York: Grove Press, 1955), pp. 357–62. Reprinted by permission.

exchanges passed by he noted down the market ratio of copper and gold; he inquired about the current quotations of the rice brokers; he sought information from druggists' and haberdashers' assistants on the state of the market at Nagasaki; for the latest news on the prices of ginned cotton, salt, and saké, he noted the various days on which the Kyoto dealers received dispatches from the Edo branch shops. Every day a thousand things were entered in his book, and people came to Fuji-ichi if they were ever in doubt. He became a valuable asset to the citizens of Kyoto.

Many traditional art forms are practiced in Japan today, pottery in particular. Japanese pottery is famous throughout the world. One of these pots may well command a price of up to $1,000. (Japan National Tourist Organization)

Invariably his dress consisted of an unlined vest next to his skin, and on top of that a cotton kimono, stuffed on occasion with three times the usual amount of padding. He never put on more than one layer of kimono. It was he who first started the wearing of detachable cuffs on the sleeves—a device both fashionable and economical. His socks were of deerskin and his clogs were fitted with high leather soles, but even so he was careful not to walk too quickly along the hard main roads. Throughout life his only silk garments were of pongee, dyed plain dark blue. There was one, it is true, which he had dyed a persistently undisguisable seaweed brown, but this was a youthful error of judgment, and he was to regret it for the next twenty years. For his ceremonial dress he had no settled crests, being content with a three-barred circle or a small conventional whirl, but even during the summer airing time he was careful to keep them from direct contact with the floor. His pantaloons were of hemp, and his starched jacket of an even tougher variety of the same cloth, so that they remained correctly creased no matter how many times he wore them.

When there was a funeral procession which his whole ward was obliged to join, he followed it perforce to the cemetery, but coming back he hung behind the others and, on the path across the moor at Rokuhara, he and his apprentices pulled up sour herbs by the roots.

"Dried in the shade," he explained, "they make excellent stomach medicine."

He never passed by anything that might be of use. Even if he stumbled he used the opportunity to pick up stones for firelighters and tucked them in his sleeve. The head of a household, if he is to keep the smoke rising steadily from his kitchen, must pay attention to a thousand things like this.

Fuji-ichi was not a miser by nature. It was merely his ambition to serve as a model for others in the management of everyday affairs. Even in the days before he made his money he never had the New Year rice cakes prepared in his own lodgings. He considered that to bother over the various utensils, and to hire a man to pound the rice, was too much trouble at such a busy time of the year; so he placed an order with the rice-cake dealer in front of the Great Buddha. However, with his intuitive grasp of good business, he insisted on paying by weight—so much per pound. Early one morning, two days before the New Year, a porter from the cake-maker, hurrying about his rounds, arrived before Fuji-ichi's shop and, setting down his load, shouted for someone to receive the order. The newly pounded cakes, invitingly arrayed, were as fresh and warm as spring itself. The master, pretending not to hear, continued his calculations on the abacus, and the cake-man, who begrudged every moment at this busy time of the year, shouted again and again. At length a young clerk, anxious to demonstrate his businesslike approach, checked the weight of the cakes on the large scales with a show of great precision, and sent the man away.

About two hours later Fuji-ichi said: "Has anyone taken in the cakes which arrived just now?"

"The man gave them to me and left long ago," said the clerk.

"Useless fellow!" cried Fuji-ichi. "I expect people in my service to have more sense! Don't you realize that you took them in before they had cooled off?"

He weighed them again, and to everyone's astonishment their weight had decreased. Not one of the cakes had been eaten, and the clerk stood gazing at them in open-mouthed amazement. . . .

In an empty space in his grounds he planted an assortment of useful trees and flowers such as willow, holly, laurel, peach, iris, and bead-beans. This he did as an education for his only daughter. Morning-glories started to grow of their own accord along the reed fence, but Fuji-ichi said that if it was a question of beauty such short-lived things were a loss, and in their place he planted runner-beans, whose flowers he thought an equally fine sight.

Nothing delighted him more than watching over his daughter. When the young girl grew into womanhood he had a marriage screen constructed for her, and since he considered

that one decorated with views of Kyoto would make her rest-
less to visit the places she had not yet seen, and that illustra-
tions of "The Tale of Genji" or "The Tales of Ise" might engender frivolous thoughts, he had the screen painted with
busy scenes of the silver and copper mines at Tada. He composed Instructional Verses on the subject of economy and
made his daughter recite them aloud. Instead of sending her to
a girls' temple school, he taught her how to write himself, and
by the time he had reached the end of his syllabus, he had
made her the most finished and accomplished girl in Kyoto.

Imitating her father in his thrifty ways, after the age of
eight she spilt no more ink on her sleeves, played no longer
with dolls at the Dolls Festival, nor joined in the dancing at
Bon [a summer festival]. Every day she combed her own hair
and bound it in a simple bun. She never sought others' help in
her private affairs. She mastered the art of stretching silk padding and learned to fit it perfectly to the length and breadth of
each garment. Since young girls can do all this if properly disciplined, it is a mistake to leave them to do as they please.

Once, on the evening of the seventh day of the New Year,
some neighbors asked leave to send their sons to Fuji-ichi's
house to seek advice on how to become millionaires. Lighting
the lamp in the sitting room, Fuji-ichi set his daughter to wait,
bidding her let him know when she heard a noise at the private
door from the street. The young girl, doing as she was told
with charming grace, first carefully lowered the wick in the
lamp. Then, when she heard the voices of the visitors, she
raised the wick again and retired to the scullery. By the time
the three guests had seated themselves the grinding of an
earthenware mortar could be heard from the kitchen, and the
sound fell with pleasant promise on their ears. They speculated
on what was in store for them.

"Pickled whaleskin soup?" hazarded the first.

"No. As this is our first visit of the year, it ought to be rice-
cake gruel," said the second.

The third listened carefully for some time, and then con-
fidently announced that it was noodle soup. Visitors always go

through this amusing performance. Fuji-ichi then entered and talked to the three of them on the requisites for success. . . .

"As a general rule," concluded Fuji-ichi, "give the closest attention to even the smallest details. Well now, you have kindly talked with me from early evening, and it is high time that refreshments were served. But not to provide refreshments is one way of becoming a millionaire. The noise of the mortar which you heard when you first arrived was the pounding of starch for the covers of the Account Book."

Steel Mill Upstate Begun by Japanese

AUBURN, N.Y., June 25 (AP)— Ground was broken in this central New York city today for a $20-million mill, the first major Japanese steel-making venture in the United States.

About two dozen Japanese business executives joined Mayor Paul W. Lattimore and other Auburn officials in turning earth on the 125-acre site of the Auburn Steel Company, Inc.

Local officials, led by Mayor Lattimore, made two trips to Japan to interest businessmen there in investing in the Auburn area, a region of above-average unemployment.

New York Times, June 26, 1973

Ethnocentrism, Japanese Style

Editor's Introduction: Sealed off from the outside world and proud of their own tradition, it was perhaps only natural that the Japanese should look with scorn at those unfortunates scattered around the world who had not been born Japanese.

Hirata Atsutane was a conservative thinker and writer of the early nineteenth century. Unlike most of his contemporaries, Hirata had read a good deal about the West. He knew something of Western medicine, astronomy, even theology. But he put his knowledge to some strange uses. For example, he read in the Christian Bible of a great flood, which was not mentioned in Japanese myths and legends. It followed, he concluded, that Japan, even though it was an island country, was higher above sea level than all those lands that were flooded in Biblical times. By "higher," of course, he also meant culturally superior.

In the first part of this reading, Hirata affirms Japan's status as the "Land of the Gods." In the second part, he attempts to misinform his readers about Dutch people. For more than 200 years, from 1640 to 1853, the Dutch were the only Westerners allowed to trade with Japan. In slandering the Dutch, Hirata is actually demeaning all Westerners.

Why does Hirata think the Japanese are superior to others? What similar arguments have you heard about the United States?

PEOPLE ALL OVER the world refer to Japan as the Land of the Gods and call us the descendants of the gods. Indeed, it is exactly as they say: our country, as a special mark of favor from the heavenly gods, was begotten by them, and there is thus so immense a difference between Japan and all the other countries of the world as to defy comparison.

Ours is a splendid and blessed country, the Land of the Gods beyond any doubt, and we, down to the most humble man and woman, are the descendants of the gods. Nevertheless, there are unhappily many people who do not understand why Japan is the land of the gods and we their descendants. . . .

Is this not a lamentable state of affairs? Japanese differ completely from and are superior to the peoples of China, India, Russia, Holland, Siam, Cambodia, and all other countries of the world, and for us to have called our country the Land of the Gods was not mere vainglory. It was the gods who formed all the lands of the world at the Creation, and these gods were without exception born in Japan.

Japan is thus the homeland of the gods, and that is why we call it the Land of the Gods. This is a matter of universal belief, and is quite beyond dispute. Even in countries where our ancient traditions have not been transmitted, the peoples recognize Japan as a divine land because of the majestic effulgence that of itself emanates from our country.

In olden days, when Korea was divided into three kingdoms, reports were heard there of how splendid, miraculous, and blessed a land Japan is, and, because Japan lies to the east of Korea, they said in awe and reverence, "To the East is a divine land, called the Land of the Rising Sun."

Word of this eventually spread all over the world, and now people everywhere refer to Japan as the Land of the Gods, irrespective of whether or not they know why this is true.*

✸   ✸   ✸

As everybody knows who has seen one, the Dutch are taller than other people, have fair complexions, big noses, and white stars in their eyes. By nature they are very light-hearted and often laugh. They are seldom angry, a fact which does not

---

* From W. de Bary, ed., *Sources of Japanese Tradition* (New York: Columbia University Press, 1958), p. 544.

The date is 1965; the place is Williamsport, Pennsylvania; the event is the Little League World Series. The umpire is an American. (United Press International)

accord with their appearance and is a seeming sign of weakness. They shave their beards, cut their nails, and are not dirty like the Chinese. Their clothing is extremely beautiful and ornamented with gold and silver.

Their eyes are really just like those of a dog. They are long from the waist downward, and the slenderness of their legs also makes them resemble animals. When they urinate they lift one leg, the way dogs do. Moreover, apparently because the backs of their feet do not reach to the ground, they fasten wooden heels to their shoes, which makes them look all the more like dogs. This may explain also why a Dutchman's penis appears to be cut short at the end, just like a dog's. This may sound like a joke, but it is quite true, not only of Dutchmen but of Russians too. . . . This may be the reason why the

Dutch are as lascivious as dogs and spend their entire nights at erotic practices. . . . Because they are thus addicted to sexual excesses and to drink, none of them lives very long. For a Dutchman to reach 50 years is as rare as for a Japanese to live to be over 100.*

‿§*Editor's Postscript:* Hirata wanted his countrymen to think of the Dutch as animals. But many Japanese were immune to his urgings. Indeed, in the late eighteenth century, an older scholar, named Otsuki, had written the following dialogue:

Q. There is a rumor that Dutchmen are short-lived. Is it true?

A. I cannot imagine where such a report originated. The length of human life is bestowed by Heaven and does not appear to differ in any country in the world. . . . Just as in Japan, the life-span of the Dutch is not the same for all. Some men live to be 100 years while others die when a bare ten or twenty years of age.

Q. People say that the Dutch are born without heels, or that their eyes are like animals', or that they are giants. Is it true?

A. Where, I wonder, do such false reports originate? Is it because their eyes differ somewhat in shape from ours that they are slandered as being animal-like? Perhaps because of the difference in continents, Europeans do differ somewhat from us Asiatics in appearance. But there is no difference whatever in the organs which they possess or their functions. . . . Even among fellow Japanese there are differences in the appearance of the eyes of people from different quarters of the country which can be recognized. In each instance the eyes thus differ a little in appearance, but the use made of them is always identical. If Japanese differ, how much more is it to be expected that people living over 20,000 miles away on a different continent should differ somewhat! Although we are all products of the same Nature, it is only to be expected that there should be regional differences in looks. As for the heels, they are the base on which the entire body rests—how could anyone get along without them? It is a subject unworthy of discussion. And as for the Dutch being giants, to judge by the height of the three men I have seen, . . . it is just as in the case of age I mentioned—some are tall and some short. . . . Moreover, stories to the effect that when Dutchmen urinate they lift one leg like dogs, or that they have many erotic arts, or that they use all kinds of aphrodisiacs are all base canards undeserving of consideration.§‿

* From Donald Keene, "Hirata Atsutane and Western Learning," *T'oung Pao,* 42:5 (1954), 374–76.

Japan Opens Line to U.S. Baseball with Entry in California League

LODI, Calif.—In the gentle, rolling hills of this agriculturally rich area 100 miles northeast of San Francisco, Japan has moved into organized baseball in the United States.

In time, Nakamura Nagayoshi, owner of the Taiheiyo Lions of the Japanese major leagues, hopes his purchase of the California League's Lodi team—the first time a foreign company has taken over a U.S. sports enterprise—will blossom into baseball on a worldwide scale, a true world series.

Boston *Globe*, August 19, 1973

An End to the Closed Society

⊸§*Editor's Introduction:* In the nineteenth century various Western governments attempted to bring Japan's policy of isolation to an end. It was the American government and its agent, Admiral Matthew C. Perry, that succeeded.

Perry arrived off the Japanese coast in 1853. He had only four ships; but even this small force was more than the Japanese could handle. The prohibition against Japanese leaving Japan and the years of seclusion had left Japan at a great disadvantage militarily.

During his first visit, Perry delivered a letter from President Millard Fillmore and explained that he would return a year later for the answer. With great reluctance, the Japanese authorities accepted Perry's documents and considered abandoning their policy of seclusion.

The following selections are taken from Perry's letter of instructions from the U.S. government and a letter of advice to the *shogun* from one Japanese leader. Why does the United States desire to end Japan's isolation? How would you characterize the American attitude? Why is the Japanese leader opposed to negotiations? How would you characterize his attitude?§⊸

Instructions to Commodore Perry

Washington, November 5, 1852

As THE SQUADRON destined for Japan will shortly be prepared to sail, I am directed by the President to explain the objects of

From *Select Documents on Japanese Foreign Policy, 1853–1868*, translated and edited by W. G. Beasley and published by Oxford University Press in 1955 for the School of Oriental and African Studies. Reprinted by permission.

the expedition, and to give some general directions as to the mode by which those objects are to be accomplished.

Since the islands of Japan were first visited by European nations, efforts have constantly been made by the various maritime powers to establish commercial intercourse with a country whose large population and reputed wealth hold out great temptations to mercantile enterprise. Portugal was the first to make the attempt, and her example was followed by Holland, England, Spain, and Russia; and finally by the United States. All these attempts, however, have thus far been unsuccessful; the permission enjoyed for a short period by the Portuguese to trade with the islands, and that granted to Holland to send annually a single vessel to the port of Nagasaki, hardly deserving to be considered exceptions to this remark.

China is the only country which carries on any considerable trade with these islands.

So rigorously is this system of exclusion carried out, that foreign vessels are not permitted to enter their ports in distress, or even to do an act of kindness to their own people. . . .

When vessels are wrecked or driven ashore on the islands their crews are subjected to the most cruel treatment. Two instances of this have recently occurred. . . .

That the civilized nations of the world should for ages have submitted to such treatment by a weak and semi-barbarous people, can only be accounted for on the supposition that, from the remoteness of the country, instances of such treatment were of rare occurrence, and the difficulty of chastising it very great. It can hardly be doubted that if Japan were situated as near the continent of Europe or of America as it is to that of Asia, its government would long since have been either treated as barbarians, or been compelled to respect those usages of civilized states of which it receives the protection. . . .

Recent events—the navigation of the ocean by steam, the acquisition and rapid settlement by this country of a vast territory on the Pacific, the discovery of gold in that region, the rapid communication established across the isthmus which separates the two oceans—have practically brought the countries of the east in closer proximity to our own; although the consequences of these events have scarcely begun to be felt, the intercourse between them has already greatly increased, and no limits can be assigned to its future extension. . . .

The objects sought by this government are—

1. To effect some permanent arrangement for the protection of American seamen and property wrecked on these islands, or driven into their ports by stress of weather.

2. The permission to American vessels to enter one or more of their ports in order to obtain supplies of provisions, water, fuel, &c., or, in case of disasters, to refit so as to enable them to prosecute their voyage. It is very desirable to have permission to establish a depot for coal, if not on one of the principal islands, at least on some small uninhabited one, of which, it is said, there are several in their vicinity.

3. The permission to our vessels to enter one or more of their ports for the purpose of disposing of their cargoes by sale or barter. . . .

The next question is, how are the above mentioned objects to be attained?

It is manifest, from past experience, that arguments or persuasion addressed to this people, unless they be seconded by some imposing manifestion of power, will be utterly unavailing.

You will, therefore, be pleased to direct the commander of the squadron to proceed, with his whole force, to such point on the coast of Japan as he may deem most advisable, and there endeavor to open a communication with the government, and, if possible, to see the emperor in person, and deliver to him the letter of introduction from the President with which he is charged. . . .

If, after having exhausted every argument and every means of persuasion, the commodore should fail to obtain from the government any relaxation of their system of exclusion, or even any assurance of humane treatment of our shipwrecked seamen, he will then change his tone, and inform them in the most unequivocal terms that it is the determination of this government to insist, that hereafter all citizens or vessels of the United States that may be wrecked on their coasts, or driven by stress of weather into their harbors shall, so long as they are compelled to remain there, be treated with humanity; and that

During Japan's long period of seclusion, it was illegal to build ships capable of crossing the ocean to China. Today, Japan is far and away the largest shipbuilding nation in the world. (Japan National Tourist Organization)

if any acts of cruelty should hereafter be practised upon citizens of this country, whether by the government or by the inhabitants of Japan, they will be severely chastised. In case he should succeed in obtaining concessions on any of the points above mentioned, it is desirable that they should be reduced into the form of a treaty, for negotiating which he will be furnished with the requisite powers.

A Japanese Leader to the Shogunate

14 August 1853

IT IS MY belief that the first and most urgent of our tasks is for the Shogunate to make its choice between peace and war. . . . I propose to give here in outline the . . . reasons why in my view we must never choose the policy of peace.

1. Although our country's territory is not extensive, foreigners both fear and respect us. That, after all, is because our resoluteness and military prowess have been clearly demonstrated to the world outside. . . . Despite this, the Americans who arrived recently, though fully aware of the Shogunate's prohibition, entered Uraga displaying a white flag as a symbol of peace and insisted on presenting their written requests. Moreover they entered Edo Bay, fired heavy guns in salute and even went so far as to conduct surveys without permission. They were arrogant and discourteous, their actions an outrage. Indeed, this was the greatest disgrace we have suffered since the dawn of our history. The saying is that if the enemy dictates terms in one's own capital one's country is disgraced. The foreigners having thus ignored our prohibition and penetrated our waters even to the vicinity of the capital, threatening us and making demands upon us, should it happen not only that the Shogunate fails to expel them but also that it concludes an agreement in accordance with their requests, then I fear it would be impossible to maintain our national prestige.

From *Select Documents on Japanese Foreign Policy, 1853–1868*, translated and edited by W. G. Beasley and published by Oxford University Press in 1955 for the School of Oriental and African Studies. Reprinted by permission.

That is the first reason why we must never choose the policy of peace. . . .

2. To exchange our valuable articles like gold, silver, copper, and iron for useless foreign goods like woollens and satin is to incur great loss while acquiring not the smallest benefit. The best course of all would be for the Shogunate to put a stop to the trade with Holland. By contrast, to open such valueless trade with others besides the Dutch would, I believe, inflict the greatest possible harm on our country. That is [another] reason why we must never choose the policy of peace.

3. For some years Russia, England, and others have sought trade with us, but the Shogunate has not permitted it. Should permission be granted to the Americans, on what grounds would it be possible to refuse if Russia and the others [again] request it? . . .

4. I hear that all, even though they be commoners, who have witnessed the recent actions of the foreigners, think them abominable; and if the Shogunate does not expel these insolent foreigners root and branch there may be some who will complain in secret, asking to what purpose have been all the preparations of gun-emplacements. It is inevitable that men should think in this way when they have seen how arrogantly the foreigners acted at Uraga. That, I believe, is because even the humblest are conscious of the debt they owe their country, and it is indeed a promising sign. Since even ignorant commoners are talking in this way, I fear that if the Shogunate does not decide to carry out expulsion, if its handling of the matter shows nothing but excess of leniency and appeasement of the foreigners, then the lower orders may fail to understand its ideas and hence opposition might arise from evil men who had lost their respect for Shogunal authority. It might even be that Shogunal control of the great lords would itself be endangered. . . .

I have tried to explain above in general terms the relative advantages and disadvantages of the war and peace policies. However, this [policy I recommend] is something that it is

easy to understand but difficult to carry out. In these feeble
days men tend to cling to peace; they are not fond of defend-
ing their country by war. They slander those of us who are
determined to fight, calling us lovers of war, men who enjoy
conflict. If matters become desperate they might, in their
enormous folly, try to overthrow those of us who are determined to fight, offering excuses to the enemy and concluding a
peace agreement with him. They would thus in the end bring
total destruction upon us. In view of our country's tradition of
military courage, however, it is probable that once the Shogunate
has taken a firm decision we shall find no such cowards among
us. But good advice is as hard to accept as good medicine is
unpleasing to the palate. A temporizing and time-serving policy is the one easiest for men to adopt. It is therefore my belief
that in this question of coast defense it is of the first importance that the Shogunate pay due heed [to these matters] and
that having once reached a decision it should never waver from
it thereafter.

The Beginnings of Change

✍§*Editor's Introduction:* Admiral Perry returned to Japan the following year, 1854. This time he had eight ships, a tiny force today but one fourth of the U.S. Navy in 1854! Perry's show of force did the trick, and he got his treaty. Japanese seclusion had come to an end.

Japan's renewed contact with the West sparked a radical upheaval in Japanese government and society. Discontented politicians blamed the government in power for Japan's military weakness. This was understandable, for that government had ruled for more than 250 years. Indeed, it had brought about Japan's isolation in the first place.

In 1868 a very different government came to power. Because in theory the new government restored power to the Emperor, this change of government is called the Meiji Restoration. (*Meiji* means enlightened rule.) In fact, however, the new government simply ruled in the name of the Emperor, for in 1868 the Emperor was only 15 years old.

Beginning in 1868, the government brought about important changes in Japan's economy, politics, and society. It fostered the development of new industries, as well as trade with the West. It promised a new form of government, which would consult those outside the government. Perhaps most important, it abolished the old system of class divisions, making samurai, farmers, and towns-

Fukuzawa Yukichi, "Gakumon no susume," in *Fukuzawa Yukichi zenshū* (Tokyo: Iwanami, 1969), III, pp. 29–31, translated by Richard H. Minear.

men legal equals. Samurai could now engage in commerce, and townsmen and farmers could enter Japan's new army.

Throughout the reforms of the Meiji government ran a new spirit, summed up best in one of its pledges of 1868: "Knowledge shall be sought throughout the world so as to strengthen the foundations of imperial rule." This openness to new ways on the part of government leaders made possible the emergence of a group of intellectuals who advocated the adoption of important aspects of Western culture. Fukuzawa Yukichi (1835–1902) was the most famous of these "Westernizers."

Prior to 1868, education beyond basic reading and writing had been open only to a few. One reason was Japan's class society. Samurai might benefit from book learning, but it was a waste of time for others—so people thought. In the first two paragraphs that follow, written in 1871, Fukuzawa discusses human equality and education. In the later passage, Fukuzawa extends his discussion from the level of individuals to the level of nations. What are his arguments for human equality? Why does he favor contact with foreign nations?&

HEAVEN DOES NOT set one man above another, nor does heaven set one man below another, so it is said. If this is so, then when Heaven gives birth to men, all men are equal. At birth there is no distinction between noble and ignoble, high and low. . . . Nevertheless, when one looks broadly at this human society of ours today, there are wise people and there are stupid ones; there are poor and there are rich; there are men of high birth and there are men of low birth. Their respective conditions are as far apart as the clouds and the mud. Why is this? The answer is very clear. [It] is a matter of whether or not they have received an education.

In pursuing an education, it is essential to know one's limitations. At birth man has no natural restrictions. Boys are boys and girls, girls. They are free and unrestricted; but if they think only of their own freedom and lack of restriction and do not know their limitations, many will become selfish and dissolute. That is, their limitation is that they should advance their own freedom based on natural principle and in accord

*The universal education Fukuzawa called for is today a reality. Japan's
literacy rate is among the world's highest, despite the great complexity
of written Japanese.* (Consulate General of Japan, N.Y.)

with human nature, without creating harm for other people.
The boundary which separates freedom from selfishness is that
between harming and not harming other people. . . .

Moreover, the matter of freedom and independence is
not merely a personal matter. It applies also to nations. Our
Japan is an island country to the east of the Asian continent.

Since antiquity, it has had no relations with foreign countries. It has clothed and fed itself solely with its own produce. Nor did it feel any insufficiency.

But since the arrival of the Americans in the 1850s, foreign trade has begun, and things have developed to their present condition. Even after the opening of the various ports, there was much dissension. There were those who clamored for closing the country off and expelling the barbarians, but their perspective was extremely narrow. They were like the proverbial frog in the well, and their assertions did not merit adoption.

The peoples of Japan and the Western nations exist in the same world, are warmed by the same sun, look up at the same moon, share the seas and share the air, and have the same human emotions. This being the case, we should hand over our surplus to them, and we should take their surplus. Without

---

**JAPANESE STUDIES
FOR U.S. BUSINESSMEN**

"North Carolina will open a business school in Raleigh in July 1981 to train U.S. businessmen in Japanese affairs as part of its efforts to lure more Japanese investment to that state. . . . Plans call for teaching U.S. businessmen the Japanese language for six months and then sending them to Japan for two years of further study."

Japan Report, June 1, 1980

shame and without pride, we should both teach each other, both learn from each other. We should assist each other and pray for each other's good fortune. We should establish ties with each other in accord with the principles of heaven and the way of man.

Japanese Imperialism
The Nineteenth Century

≈§Editor's Introduction: The last reading dealt with the cultural impact of the West on Japan. The West also had an enormous effect on other aspects of Japanese life. For example, Japan was forced to sign treaties that gave Western nations and their citizens special privileges in Japan. Nevertheless, Japan was not colonized by the West. In fact, Japan herself soon joined the ranks of the exploiters.

Many factors led Japan, in the years after 1868, to attempt to extend her influence in Asia. For one thing, Japan experienced a growing need for raw materials. For another, Japan's success in modernizing her society seemed to many Japanese to justify taking an active role in "modernizing" the rest of Asia. Many Japanese leaders were all too ready to judge other cultures by Japanese standards and to find these other cultures inferior.

We see some of these factors at work in the next selection, by Fukuzawa Yukichi, whose ideas on equality, education, and international relations were presented in the last reading. Only a very few years after writing that essay, Fukuzawa sang a very different tune. If a man like Fukuzawa can support imperialist policies, we can expect to find very little opposition among Japanese to the creation of a Japanese empire.§≈

From Carmen Blacker, *The Japanese Enlightenment* (Cambridge, England: Cambridge University Press, 1964), pp. 129–236. Reprinted by permission.

IT IS NOT long since the foreigners came to our country, and up till now they have not had time to harm or disgrace us very much, so that most people are not particularly worried about them. But those who truly have their country's welfare at heart must judge the foreigners by what they have done and are doing in the rest of the world.

To whom did the present America once belong? The Red Indians, who were originally masters of the country, were driven out by the white men, so that the position of host and guest has entirely changed. The civilization of America is thus not really America's at all, but the white man's.

And besides, what about the various Eastern countries and the Pacific Islands? Have the European countries really respected the rights and interests and integrity of the countries with which they have come into contact? . . . The Sandwich Islands [Hawaii] since their discovery by Captain Cook in 1778 are said to have progressed in civilization much more quickly than the neighboring islands. But their population, which was 3,400,000 when they were discovered, had dropped to 140,000 by 1823—so that in the space of fifty years the population had decreased each year by 8 per cent.

. . . What exactly is this thing known as "civilization"? For the people of these islands it meant that they gave up the bad custom of cannibalism, but also that they became slaves of the white man. In the case of an enormous country like China, the white men have not yet been able to penetrate into the interior and have left their mark only on the coast—but it looks very much as though in the future the Chinese Empire will become European territory.

Wherever the Europeans come, the land ceases to be productive, and trees and plants cease to grow. Worse still, the human race sometimes dies out. If people understand these things clearly, and at the same time realize that Japan is an Eastern country, they must inevitably fear for the future, even though up till now Japan has suffered no great harm from foreign intercourse. (1876)

❀   ❀   ❀

Western nations call themselves "Christian nations" and make a clear distinction between themselves and everyone else. The word "nations" in their so-called Law of Nations does not refer to all the nations in the world, but only to those that happen to be Christian.

The Law of Nations has never been seen to operate in non-Christian countries. It is thus something based entirely on custom and sentiment. . . .

There are some Western scholars, certainly, who deplore this and advocate a truly fair and impartial Law of Nations, but in practice it usually works out in the very opposite way. Take, for example, the cruel way in which the British have ruled the Indians for some years past. . . . But if one says that the Indians are treated in this way simply because they are weak, it should follow that the many weak countries in the West would also be treated in the same cruel way. The fact that they are not treated in this way proves that it is not differences in strength but differences in race and kind which are the cause of differences in treatment. Indeed, if it should happen that one of the small countries of their own kind should suffer calamity, someone will always go to their aid.

This is what they call the Balance of Power. Some people try to maintain that the Balance of Power is governed by considerations of political advantage, but this is not to be believed. What really underlies it in practice is the sentiment men bear towards people of their own kind. For whatever excesses Westerners may commit in Eastern countries, no one would dream of lifting a finger against them. (1881)

❉   ❉   ❉

Since ancient times it has been the custom for countries to make treaties with each other. These documents always profess in the most solemn terms principles of friendship between the two countries. But what is the point, may I ask, of such solemn and high-sounding principles? . . . Nations are just like merchants, who care only for profit and give no thought to duty, and who exchange contracts with each other only to watch for the first opportunity of breaking them. Merchants, however, will hesitate to break their bonds for fear of proceedings in a law court. But there is no law court in the world to deal with broken bonds between nations. Thus the factor deciding whether promises shall be kept or not, and whether treaties possess authority or not, is the relative wealth and strength of the two countries. . . .

But the point I am trying to make now is that our country is in the greatest danger. Moralists may tell us to sit back and wait for the day when war will cease, but as I see it the Western countries have already greatly developed their military techniques and are likely to develop them even further in future. Lately they have been inventing new and curious weapons every day, and their armies have been daily increasing in size.

All this may be useless and stupid, but when others treat one stupidly one can only do the same back to them. When others use violence, we must be violent too. When others use

---

The Rising Sun and the Lone Star

Production is being stepped up this year at the San Angelo plant of Mitsubishi Aircraft International, Inc., a subsidiary of Mitsubishi Heavy Industries, Ltd., where executive turboprop airplanes selling in the $450,000–$600,000 price range are made.

Mitsubishi took over the factory, which had been operated by the Mooney Aircraft Company, in 1969. Factory production increased to 47 aircraft last year from 30 in 1971. Factory deliveries last year were 64, up from 39 in 1971. Kuroiwa Makoto, president of the Texas plant, supervises the assembly and wiring work that is done at the San Angelo facility. The plant employs 258 Texans.

New York Times, February 18, 1973

deceitful trickery we must do likewise. And when one is taken up with stupidity, violence, and trickery one has no time to think of right and proper moral behavior. I said before somewhere that nationalism was a temporary expedient—but I confess myself to be a supporter of this expedient. (1881)

*   *   *

We cannot wait for our neighbor countries to become so civilized that all may combine together to make Asia progress. We must rather break out of formation and behave in the same way as the civilized countries of the West are doing. . . . We would do better to treat China and Korea in the same way as do the Western nations. (1885)

Imperial Japan, 1940

Editor's Introduction: Fukuzawa wrote in 1885 that Japan should treat China and Korea "in the same way as do the Western nations." He meant that Japan should impose her will on them, if necessary by force. Only ten years later Japan began to do just that.

In 1894–95 Japan went to war with China to determine which would control Korea. To secure the same goal, control of Korea, Japan fought Russia in 1904–05. In both wars, Japan was the victor.

By the outbreak of World War I, the Japanese empire included Taiwan, won from China in 1895; Korea, annexed outright in 1910; and some economic control of Manchuria. This empire remained relatively stable into the 1930s, when Japan set up a puppet government in Manchuria (1932), expanded her area of control into North China, and stumbled into a major war against China (1937–45). In 1941 Japan added the United States and the Western Allies to the list of her opponents.

In June, 1940, Arita Hachiro, Foreign Minister of Japan, delivered the following radio address. What are his goals? How would you react to them if you were Chinese or Korean or Vietnamese?

. . . It SEEMS TO be a most natural step that peoples who are closely related to each other geographically, racially, culturally, and economically should first form a sphere of their own

Foreign Relations of the United States: Japan, 1931–1941 (Washington, D.C.: U.S. Government Printing Office, 1943), Vol. II, pp. 93–94.

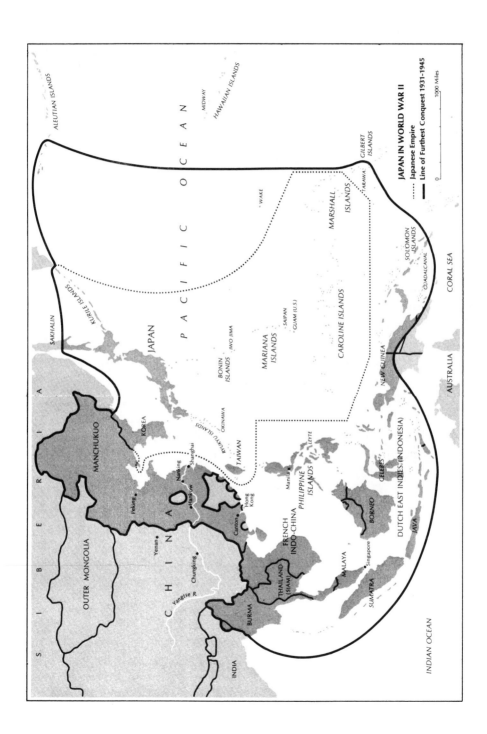

JAPAN IN WORLD WAR II
▓ Japanese Empire
▪▪▪ Line of Furthest Conquest 1931-1945

1000 Miles

ALEUTIAN ISLANDS

PACIFIC OCEAN

MIDWAY

HAWAIIAN ISLANDS

GILBERT
ISLANDS

TARAWA

WAKE

MARSHALL
ISLANDS

SOLOMON
ISLANDS

GUADALCANAL

CORAL SEA

SAKHALIN

KURILE ISLANDS

JAPAN

SAIPAN

GUAM (U.S.)

MARIANA
ISLANDS

CAROLINE ISLANDS

BONIN
ISLANDS

IWO JIMA

NEW GUINEA

AUSTRALIA

S I B E R I A

MANCHUKUO

KOREA

OKINAWA

RYUKYU ISLANDS

TAIWAN

LEYTE

PHILIPPINE
ISLANDS

Manila

CELEBES

Peking

C H I N A

Nanking

Shanghai

Hankow

Hong
Kong

Canton

FRENCH
INDO-CHINA

BORNEO

DUTCH EAST INDIES (INDONESIA)

JAVA

OUTER MONGOLIA

Yenan

Chungking

Yangtse R.

THAILAND
(SIAM)

MALAYA

Singapore

SUMATRA

BURMA

INDIA

INDIAN OCEAN

for coexistence and coprosperity and establish peace and order within that sphere, and at the same time secure a relationship of common existence and prosperity with other spheres.
The cause of strife which mankind has hitherto experienced
lies generally in the failure to give due consideration to the
necessity of some such natural and constructive world order
and to remedy old irrationalities and injustices. . . .

It is in this spirit that Japan is now engaged in the task of
establishing a new order in East Asia. It is extremely regrettable, therefore, that there should be those who not only fail
to understand Japan's great undertaking based upon this fundamental principle but, on the contrary, obstruct establishment
of peace in East Asia by supporting the regime of Chiang Kai-
shek. We have urged them to reconsider such an attitude in the
past, and now we intend further to urge their serious reflec-
tion. We are determined to leave no stone unturned in order
to eradicate all activities for assisting Chiang Kai-shek.

Sometimes there are those who would disapprove a change
in the *status quo* by force of arms regardless of the reasons
therefor. It is for the purpose of bringing about a just and
permanent peace that Japan has been fighting in China for the
past three years. Her employment of armed force is an act looking beyond the immediate present. The sword she has drawn is
intended to be nothing other than a life-giving sword that de-
stroys evil and makes justice manifest.

Countries of East Asia and regions of the South Seas are
geographically, historically, racially, and economically very
closely related to each other. They are destined to help each
other and minister to one another's needs for their common
well-being and prosperity, and to promote peace and progress
in their regions. Uniting of all these regions under a single
sphere on the basis of common existence and insuring thereby
the stability of that sphere is, I think, a natural conclusion. The
idea to establish first a righteous peace in each of the various
regions and then establish collectively a just peace for the
whole world has long existed also in Europe and America.

This system presupposes the existence of a stabilizing

force in each region, with which as a center the peoples within that region are to secure their coexistence and coprosperity and as well the stability of their sphere. It also presupposes that these groups will respect [one] another's individual characteristics, political, cultural, and economic, and they will cooperate and fulfill one another's needs for their common good. . . .

Japan, while carrying on vigorously her task of constructing a new order in East Asia, is paying serious attention to developments in the European war and to its repercussions in the various quarters of East Asia, including the South Seas [Southeast Asia] region. I desire to declare that the destiny of these regions in any development therein, and any disposal thereof, is a matter of grave concern to Japan in view of her mission and responsibility as the stabilizing force in East Asia.

World War II

❧Editor's Introduction: Only eighteen months after Foreign Minister Arita's address, the Japanese empire collided head-on with the United States. Japan's attack on Pearl Harbor precipitated the Pacific War; it also brought the United States into active involvement in World War II in Europe.

What lay behind the war? The issues were not simple, and even today we have no definitive answers. In the following essay an American historian explores some aspects of the road to Pearl Harbor. Why did the Japanese leaders decide to attack?❧

ON DECEMBER 7, 1941, a strike force of the Japanese Navy launched a surprise attack on the American naval base at Pearl Harbor, in Hawaii. The effect was devastating: four battleships sunk and four damaged; 230 planes destroyed or heavily damaged; 2,400 dead and 1,300 wounded. The attack brought the United States into World War II. It unified Americans in opposition to the Japanese war aims. It reinforced the widespread belief that the Japanese were not to be trusted.

The Japanese leaders had not expected the attack on Pearl Harbor to have these effects. They had hoped, instead, that a sudden crippling blow would break the American will to resist. What were the issues at stake between the United States and Japan in 1941?

By Richard H. Minear.

During the 1920s the Japanese had pursued a policy of co-operating with the other great powers in Asia. But in the 1930s the Japanese became disillusioned with the policy of coopera-tion, convinced that it did not afford sufficient protection for their national interest. For this reason they decided to go it alone, to secure by whatever means necessary the sphere of influence to which they felt entitled.

That sphere of influence was not restricted to the main islands of Japan. The home islands were woefully deficient in raw materials. Hence, from the very early stages of Japan's de-fense planning, it was apparent that Korea and Manchuria must be incorporated economically into the Japanese empire. Similarly, the countries of Southeast Asia, with their rubber

Along "battleship row" in Pearl Harbor lie the USS West Virginia, the USS Tennessee, and the USS Arizona (sunk in the attack on December 7, 1941). (Wide World Photos)

and oil, attracted Japanese attention. Thus, Japan's planning for national security presupposed an area of control far beyond the territorial confines of the Japan we know today—in effect, a Japanese version of the Monroe Doctrine.

There were other factors in Japanese planning. Most Japanese leaders were strongly anti-Communist, and they feared the spread of Russian influence into Asia. China was absorbed in a civil war. The spectre of a Communist victory in China caused nightmares for Japanese planners; and even without so dire a prospect, continued instability in China seemed to threaten Japan's interests.

The growth of American power in the Pacific was another major factor. What, wondered the Japanese, were the real intentions of the Americans? Why was the United States intent on expanding her naval power? Why was she adamant in her support of China against Japan?

For their part, the Americans really had no well-thought-out Asian policy. A long tradition of contacts with China (including a large missionary effort) and an instinctive sympathy for the underdog combined with American fears of Japanese power in the Pacific led the United States to support China. Japan's alliance with Nazi Germany in fact never amounted to much, but it greatly alarmed the United States. The final straw was Japan's military action in China and, in 1940–41, Indochina.

For all its economic and military power in the 1930s, Japan had an Achilles heel: oil. Japan in 1941 produced just over 10 per cent of her *peacetime* oil needs. The other 90 per cent had to be imported. The bulk of Japan's imports (80 per cent) came from the United States, whose oil production was 700 times greater than Japan's.

The United States responded to Japan's move into southern Indochina by cutting off all oil shipments to Japan (July, 1941). This action brought issues to a head: Either the Japanese would back down, or they would take military action to secure their own supplies of oil.

The Japanese chose not to back down. On December 7, 1941, Japan invaded Southeast Asia and simultaneously struck at Pearl Harbor. The decision to go to war was taken with great reluctance. Here are the words of the Japanese Prime Minister, Tojo, at the end of a crucial government conference (November 5, 1941):

> If we enter into a protracted war, there will be difficulties. . . . The first stage of the war will not be difficult. We have some uneasiness about a protracted war. But how can we let the United States continue to do as she pleases, even though there is some uneasiness? Two years from now we will have no petroleum for military use. Ships will stop moving. When I think about the strengthening of American defenses in the Southwest Pacific, the expansion of the American fleet, the unfinished China Incident [Japan's war with China], and so on, I see no end to difficulties.*

The war did become "protracted." Japan soon lost the initiative. America brought her vastly superior power to bear, and Japan's fate was sealed.

Thirty-three years after Pearl Harbor, historians have begun to question the wisdom of American policy in the prewar period. Why was the United States hostile to Japanese expansion in the 1930s? This question has a special sting, for in the postwar years the United States has supported actively Japanese economic penetration of Southeast Asia. What was the American national interest in 1941? Would a softer line with the Japanese have avoided war in 1941 and yet protected America's basic interests?

Were the Allies wise in taking the decision to cut off Japan's supplies of oil? Were no less drastic remedies available? In the fall of 1973, the American people first awoke to their own energy crisis, as fighting in the Middle East erupted. The parallel with Japan's energy crisis of 1941 is far from exact, but perhaps it will lead to a re-evaluation of America's policy and Japan's response.

These issues will not be settled for many years. What does seem clear about the road to Pearl Harbor is this: For reasons

---

* Nobutaka Ike, ed., *Japan's Decision for War* (Stanford: Stanford University Press, 1967), p. 230.

of national security the Japanese attempted to gain a dominant position in Asia. In the 1930s, when China was turned inward and Russia was only beginning to develop her Asian strength, this goal was not an unrealistic one. However, the United States placed herself squarely in the path of Japanese ambitions. The result was the Japanese attack on Pearl Harbor and the war that followed it.

U.S.-Japan Joint Venture Builds Oil Transport System

The Foreign Investment Council of the Ryukyu government has approved the creation of a new enterprise which plans to construct the biggest oil central transportation system (CTS) in the world.

The new enterprise is Okinawa Kyodo Oil Terminals, Inc. which will be formed jointly with equal investments by the Kyodo Oil Co. of Japan and the Gulf Oil Corp. of the U.S.

Japan Report, July, 1972

Two Imperial Rescripts

~§*Editor's Introduction:* The Japanese Emperor, Hirohito, had little influence on the decision to go to war in 1941. If anything, he leaned toward peace. At one point, he expressed his views by quoting a poem written by his grandfather, the Emperor Meiji: "Since all are brothers in this world/ Why is there such constant turmoil?" But once his ministers had made up their minds, Hirohito gave his seal of approval to their decision. His countrymen learned of that decision in the Imperial Rescript, or proclamation, reprinted below.

Four years later, the Japanese government surrendered. In this second decision the Emperor played a very active role, in effect ordering his ministers to accept the Allies' demand for surrender. Again, his countrymen learned of the decision in an Imperial Rescript.

Needless to say, these rescripts present only one side of a very complex picture. What are the war goals stated in the first rescript? What does the Emperor ask of his subjects? What reasons for surrender are stated in the second rescript? What does the Emperor then ask of his subjects?§~

Declaring War on the U.S.A. and Britain

December 7, 1941

WE, BY GRACE of heaven, Emperor of Japan, seated on the throne of a line unbroken for ages eternal, enjoin upon ye, Our loyal and brave subjects:

Iichiro Tokutomi, *The Imperial Rescript Declaring War on the United States and British Empire.* Tokyo, 1942.

91

We hereby declare war on the United States of America and the British Empire. The men and officers of Our army and navy shall do their utmost in prosecuting the war. Our public servants of various departments shall perform faithfully and diligently their appointed tasks, and all other subjects of Ours shall pursue their respective duties; the entire nation with a united will shall mobilize their total strength so that nothing will miscarry in the attainment of our war aims.

To insure the stability of East Asia and to contribute to world peace is the farsighted policy which was formulated by Our Great Illustrious Imperial Grandsire [the Meiji Emperor] and Our Great Imperial Sire succeeding Him, and which We lay constantly to heart.

To cultivate friendship among nations and to enjoy prosperity in common with all nations has always been the guiding principle of Our Empire's foreign policy. It has been truly unavoidable and far from Our wishes that Our Empire has now been brought to cross swords with America and Britain.

More than four years have passed since China, failing to comprehend the true intentions of Our Empire, and recklessly courting trouble, disturbed the peace of East Asia and compelled Our Empire to take up arms. Although there has been re-established the National Government of China, with which Japan had effected neighborly intercourse and cooperation, the regime which has survived at Chungking, relying upon American and British protection, still continues its fratricidal opposition.

Eager for the realization of their inordinate ambition to dominate the Orient, both America and Britain, giving support to the Chungking regime, have aggravated the disturbances in East Asia.

Moreover, these two Powers, inducing other countries to follow suit, increased military preparations on all sides of Our Empire to challenge us. They have obstructed by every means our peaceful commerce, and finally resorted to a direct severance of economic relations, menacing gravely the existence of Our Empire.

Patiently have We waited and long have We endured in the hope that Our Government might retrieve the situation in peace, but Our adversaries, showing not the least spirit of conciliation, have unduly delayed a settlement, and in the meantime they have intensified the economic and political pressure to compel thereby Our Empire to submission.

This trend of affairs would, if left unchecked, not only nullify Our Empire's efforts of many years to stabilize East Asia, but also endanger the very existence of Our nation. The situation being as it is, Our Empire for its existence and self-defense has no other recourse but to appeal to arms and to crush every obstacle in its path.

The hallowed spirits of Our Imperial Ancestors guarding Us from above, We rely upon the loyalty and courage of Our subjects in Our confident expectation that the task bequeathed by Our Forefathers will be carried forward, and that the source of evil will be speedily eradicated and an enduring peace immutably established in East Asia, preserving thereby the glory of Our Empire.

Announcing Japan's Surrender

August 14, 1945

To Our good and loyal subjects:

After pondering deeply the general trends of the world and the actual conditions obtaining in Our Empire today, We have decided to effect a settlement of the present situation by resorting to an extraordinary measure.

We have ordered Our Government to communicate to the governments of the United States, Great Britain, China, and the Soviet Union that Our Empire accepts the provisions of their Joint Declaration [Potsdam Declaration].

To strive for the common prosperity and happiness of all nations as well as the security and well-being of Our subjects is the solemn obligation which has been handed down by Our

Imperial Ancestors, and which We lay close to heart. Indeed, We declared war on America and Britain out of Our sincere desire to ensure Japan's self-preservation and the stabilization of East Asia, it being far from Our thought either to infringe upon the sovereignty of other nations or to embark upon territorial aggrandizement. But now the war has lasted for nearly four years. Despite the best that has been done by everyone— the gallant fighting of military and naval forces, the diligence and assiduity of Our servants of the State, and the devoted service of Our 100,000,000 people, the war situation has developed not necessarily to Japan's advantage, while the general trends of the world have all turned against her interest.

On September 2, 1945, representatives of the Japanese government stand stiffly at attention at the surrender ceremonies on the battleship USS Missouri, anchored in Tokyo Bay. (Wide World Photos)

Moreover, the enemy has begun to employ a new and most cruel bomb, the power of which to do damage is indeed incalculable, taking the toll of many innocent lives. Should We continue to fight, it would result not only in the ultimate collapse and obliteration of the Japanese nation but also in the total extinction of human civilization. Such being the case, how are We to save the millions of Our subjects or to atone Ourselves before the hallowed spirits of Our Imperial Ancestors? This is the reason We have ordered the acceptance of the provisions of the Joint Declaration of the Powers.

We cannot but express the deepest sense of regret to our Allied nations of East Asia, who have consistently cooperated with the Empire toward the emancipation of East Asia. The thought of those officers and men as well as others who have fallen in the fields of battle, those who died at their posts of duty, or those who met with untimely death and all their bereaved families pains Our heart night and day. The welfare of the wounded and the war-sufferers, and of those who have lost their homes and livelihood, are the objects of Our profound solicitude. The hardships and sufferings to which Our nation is to be subjected hereafter will be certainly great. We are keenly aware of the inmost feelings of all ye, Our subjects. However, it is according to the dictate of time and fate that We have resolved to pave the way for a grand peace for all the generations to come by enduring the unendurable and suffering what is insufferable.

Having been able to safeguard and maintain the structure of the Imperial State, We are always with ye, Our good and loyal subjects, relying upon your sincerity and integrity. Beware most strictly of any outbursts of emotion which may engender needless complications, or any fraternal contention and strife which may create confusion, lead ye astray, and cause ye to lose the confidence of the world. Let the entire nation continue as one family from generation to generation, ever firm in its faith in the imperishability of its divine land, and mindful of its heavy burden of responsibilities and the

long road before it. Unite your total strength to be devoted
to the construction for the future. Cultivate the way of recti-
tude, foster nobility of spirit, and work with resolution so that
ye may enhance the innate glory of the Imperial State and
keep pace with the progress of the world.

Ichiro's Diary

PART I

⋙*Editor's Introduction:* How does it feel to lose a major war? How does it feel to have bombs dropping around you? In the following selection we learn of the reaction of one Japanese, Hatano Ichiro. During the war years Ichiro was in his teens. For most of that time Ichiro exchanged a series of letters and diary entries with his mother.

Being a teenager is not easy in the best of times. In wartime it is doubly difficult. Like anyone else, Ichiro strives to conform. At school this means accepting the patriotic mood, the war, and the official reasons for fighting. After all, we all want to be patriotic.

At home, however, Ichiro encounters a very different atmosphere. His father, a professor and writer, is critical of the war on political grounds. His mother, a journalist, deeply resents the inhuman suffering the war has brought. However, she is also most sympathetic to Ichiro's problem: how to resolve the tensions he feels, how to discover true patriotism.

For a brief period at the beginning of the war, he was separated from his family, remaining in Tokyo and going to school there while his parents and brothers moved to a rural town perhaps 100 miles distant.

Most experts now agree that Japan's defeat was inevitable by May of 1944, the day of Ichiro's first letter. However, it was not until at least a year later that this reality became apparent to many Japanese.

Isoko and Ichiro Hatano, *Mother and Son* (Boston: Houghton Mifflin, 1962), pp. 7–8, 10–12, 70–72, 75–76, 82–83, 84–85, 89–90, 91–92.

Where do Ichiro's sympathies lie? How do they change as the war develops?

From Ichiro to His Mother

May 17, 1944

WHAT BOTHERS ME . . . are the bombings. Do you really think there will be any? They say that enemy aircraft will definitely not be allowed to get as far as Tokyo, so perhaps there will be no danger. Whenever the air-raid warning siren goes off, we are immediately sent home from school. What should I do if things seem to be going really badly? Go down into the shelter or go to the Fujiis' house? Their shelter is made of concrete and very safe. In any case, as soon as I hear the actual air-raid siren, I will certainly hurry quickly onto a train and go to you. If the train is bombed during the journey—well, that will be the end of that. When the alert lasts three days, like last time, you feel as though you will never breathe again.

May 23, 1944

. . . Another thing, Mother: you cried today at Fujisawa, didn't you, when from the train window we saw all those soldiers leaving? I don't like you to cry like that, just anywhere. The people opposite us were looking at you. And although you knew none of the soldiers, you said: "Oh, they are all going off so full of enthusiasm!" I was terribly embarrassed.

Those soldiers are glad to go, Mother. They are going for their country's sake. If they are killed, nothing can be done about it. Later on, I shall go away like that. I've never really thought about dying for His Majesty the Emperor, perhaps because I have not once been close enough to see him; but if it is for my country, I am ready to die at any time. Don't you think that is right?

It seems you are not capable of becoming a wartime mother. Poor Mother, I love you so very much; but in this one matter I simply cannot admire you. Perhaps it is unjust to say this, but would you be less brave than the wife of the grocer who lives at the bottom of the hill, or the wife of the tinker [repairman] who lives near the temple of Hikawa? This thought makes me terribly unhappy.

To Ichiro from His Mother

May 24, 1944

Your letter of yesterday touched me on a sore spot.

I am sorry about what happened at Fujisawa. But when I caught sight of those young men, it made me very sad to see them so full of enthusiasm. Each one of them has a mother who has gone through untold pain in trying to bring up her children well. These mothers must now witness without protest their sons being led off to war. When I thought of the sorrow of these women, I could not hold back my tears. As you say, I am not brave. I realize this is a weakness. But do you think there is anyone in the world who would not be sad to see a son leave for the war? Isn't it rather that people force themselves to look happy, although in their hearts they are unbearably miserable? To my mind there is nothing wrong in expressing your sadness honestly if you really are sad. Isn't it enough to resign yourself afterwards?

You will certainly not be satisfied with this way of thinking. I understand that too. All the same, you will probably come to agree with me more when you are a little older. Or at least you will not despise me.

At the end of July Ichiro decides to leave Tokyo, and join his family in the country, because "if I were killed while alone here in Tokyo, it would make you so unhappy." Even when they are united, however, he continues to write to his mother.

One thing that bothers Ichiro is the need to buy food on the black market to supplement the meager rations allowed by the government. Not only does he object to the illegality of the practice; he is also embarrassed by his friends' knowing that his family is using the black market. It is for this reason that he asks his mother to make a detour on her buying trips to avoid the house of a friend (near the Miyako-za).

A few days later, when fourteen-year-old Ichiro himself does the buying, he learns the painful lesson of having to swallow one's pride for the sake of survival.

From Ichiro to His Mother

December 18, 1944

Please forgive me for having made such a fuss about the food-buying the other day. When I tried it myself today I

Two decades after 1944, the Ichiros of today have very different things on their minds. Here a young bowler polishes his form while waiting for a bus. (UPI Photo)

realized how agonizing it was. Please don't bother ever again about what my friends might say. I don't care at all if you pass the Miyako-za Cinema.

When I left home this morning I felt very pleased to be going in your place; but once I got to the farmer's, I found them so arrogant that I was flabbergasted. If it's like that even when they know you, what must it be like when you go to them for the first time! It still makes me hot just to think of having to beg from those country bumpkins. We are not begging but buying, and that at absolutely frightful prices!

I almost lost my temper, but I managed to control myself by thinking that if I let myself go, you would have to dash all over the place looking for new farms. As far as I'm concerned, it doesn't really matter; but it brings tears of anger to my eyes to think of you lowering yourself to such people.

I know what it is like to be hungry, but, Mother, try to ask these people for things as seldom as possible, even if it's only a few times less, since I would rather go about with an empty stomach. I wouldn't complain.

They said to me: "The price had better be good!" It is they who stand on their dignity, it is they who look as though they are doing me a favor, and yet all they give me is a few measly pumpkins and potatoes. And then I have to put them on my bicycle and carry them home under the hostile looks of all the local people. . . .

Today has taught me a good deal. At the time it all made me feel angry and almost ready to cry; but now I'm glad that I have had the chance, at least once, to share your troubles. . . .

From your Ichiro,
who has grown up a little during the day

To Ichiro from His Mother

January, 1945

Toward midday a member of the secret police came to the house. (The secret police is the branch which deals with the repression of subversive ideas.) This man has been at the house twice before and I was not terribly surprised to see him come; but yesterday his manner of questioning was particularly violent. Your father had done nothing wrong, but the police probably have their eye on him because they consider him a "liberal."

I don't know where they have picked up the idea, but they maintain that morale is very low among the soldiers who have gone through the University and that this is the fault of bad teaching by the professors.

He asked where your father went yesterday, if he often talked to the members of the neighborhood group, and the like.

He seems to consider your father a man of considerable influence.

Haven't I told you again and again that it is not true that your father has no worries? If he doesn't go to the group meetings and the ration distributions it is partly because he does not like that sort of thing and does not know how to go about it, but also, I think, because he has worries such as yesterday's incident. Your father is so made that he will say exactly what he thinks when asked for his opinion of the present tide of war and this obviously will not do him any good.

But if things go on as they are now, it is probable that he will sooner or later be taken in by the police, on one pretext or another. That is what we were brooding about yesterday. And even if this is still only a remote eventuality, there is always the possibility of his being called into the army.

⊸§Bombs fell on Tokyo beginning in late 1944. On March 9, 1945, American firebombs killed 73,000 people—mostly civilians—and leveled 16 square miles of the city. Tokyo escaped the atom bomb, but the devastation of the city on this day was greater than that at Hiroshima or Nagasaki.

For those who have left the cities, like Ichiro and his family, falling bombs are a less common sight. Ichiro's first experience comes in February, 1945.§⊶

From Ichiro to His Mother

February 16, 1945

So now Suwa has been bombed—for the first time since we came here. I don't know if you saw the airplanes but, from our shelter in the mountains, we easily made out the B-29's as they flew over leaving long trails of white behind.

As it was the first time I had seen them, they seemed almost beautiful rather than terrifying. Yet I can hardly contain myself when I remember that these machines are devastating our country and may soon destroy Tokyo. As to Suwa, as long as we were saved, I would almost not mind if such a place and all its spiteful people were razed to the ground. . . .

Of the boys at school, Naito is going to try to get into the

Military Academy and several of my friends are trying for the Officers' Training School. I knew you would be against it, so I haven't said anything until now; but I would like to try for one of these schools, although it worries me that I might not be fit enough. It's all very well hurling bamboo spears at the B-29's, but it won't have much effect on them. I too have Japanese blood in my veins.

March 6, 1945

Dearest Mother,

You have not written me for some time. Every day I open this notebook, but I never find anything.

I know how very busy you are, and I don't want to be a nuisance, but do try to write. Nowadays, I no longer know what I ought to do. You are the only one left to guide me. Please help.

I want to do what's right. But I am unable to find out where the truth lies.

Our teacher says that we should make every sacrifice for the good of the war. My friends say so too. But doesn't Father say just the opposite? And it's not only Father. You agree with him, don't you?

If it were only Father who said these things, I could take no notice of them. But you think as he does, so I am forced to believe it is the truth. This is what worries me.

Please show me what is right, Mother. I wish you would tell me, quite impartially, what you think about these things.

I envy the people who can go and fight the enemy without any hesitation.

Your Ichiro, at his wits' end

To Ichiro from His Mother

I am a bad mother not to have written you. But you know that I have been terribly busy in the evening working on articles.

I noticed what was going on in your mind long before you

told me. I find it completely natural and understandable, and I am of course full of sympathy for you. Nevertheless, my answer is: wait another six months [before enlisting]. If six months is too long, three months. Wait three months and things will become clearer to you.

I too have learned a great deal and I would not want to protect your body at the expense of your soul. If I cannot act like a "patriotic" mother, I can at least act as befits the mother of a boy who is as fair-minded as you are. But please wait a little longer, just a little longer.

The three months Ichiro's mother asked him to wait before enlisting are critical ones for Japan. The devastation of Japan continues, and Germany surrenders. Japan and Germany had been formally allied, but throughout the war their alliance had been of very little benefit to either country, for the two "allies" had gone their independent ways. The Allies focused their efforts first on defeating Germany. With Germany out of the war, Japan faces the full wrath of the Allied forces.

Ichiro, now fifteen years old, finds his thoughts changing.

From Ichiro to His Mother

May 8, 1945

Dearest Mother,

Father was right after all. Germany has ended by losing. I don't suppose this surprised Father at all, but most other people seem rather worried. This means that Japan will have to fight the whole world alone. And it is only a matter of time before we will be defeated, isn't it? People are saying: "Now we will show what we are made of," but they are unable to hide their fears. The war has turned out as Father foretold; his view was the right one. I shall no longer badger you for impossible things, like going to the Officers' Training School.

But when will the war end and how will it end? Is it really a case of "kill or be killed," and if we lose, will we all be slaughtered? When I thought that there was something splendid about our fighting, the idea of death didn't frighten me much. But now it just seems absurd.

They say our soldiers have done some horrible things in China and elsewhere.

Father looks relieved, which could get him into trouble if people noticed. Tell him to be careful.

May 12, 1945

Dearest Mother,

Today I have something important to tell you.

The war is becoming more violent and nobody knows when it will end. Moreover, who knows what may happen to Father from one day to the next? And finally, I can't bear to see you going in search of food every day when you hardly eat anything yourself.

That is why—and I have thought it over very carefully—I plan to leave school at the end of term.

I well know that if you have taken so much trouble over my education, it is not so that I might become a farmer. I am not at all eager to give up lessons myself, and I hate to think of meeting my friends who are still at school. But when I see your tired face, I just can't worry about such silly things.

There have been loads of famous men who never went to school, and anyway, at the present moment, it is more important to stay alive than to try to be a great man.

I don't think I would be able to work in the rice fields yet, but I believe I could handle the others. I could also go to the mountains to get wood. And if we manage to get some eggs hatched at the neighbors', I could easily raise chickens. And you wouldn't have to bother any longer about my daily lunch basket. You never say anything, but it breaks my heart to see how you struggle to get something tasty for me every day. It is really too idiotic that we, who led a decent life in Tokyo, must now accept these peasants' insults and their sneers about our being "refugees," and are forced to barter fine clothing for almost nothing just so they can dress up their nasty wives, who might barely pass for good-looking among the savages of the Pacific islands. . . .

Ichiro's Diary

PART II

~§*Editor's Introduction:* The first group of selections from Ichiro's diary traced his changing emotions as Japan faced bombardment, then defeat. He had never been an enthusiastic supporter of the war, although he did speak at one time of dropping out of school to enlist.

For Japan and for Ichiro, the end comes in August, 1945. On August 6 the first atom bomb falls on Hiroshima. At the time no one knows what has happened. The following diary entries trace Ichiro's initial inability to grasp the truth, his horror when he finally learns it, and his reaction to the news that Japan has surrendered.

How does the defeat affect him? How does it affect his image of the enemy—the United States?§~

August 7, 1945

They say that Hiroshima has been bombed and there has been frightful damage. From what I heard on the radio, I believed the raid to be quite a localized one. But Kinji says it might be what is called an "atom" bomb. It seems that these bombs are a new and extraordinarily powerful weapon and kill every living thing in the area. I began by telling Kinji, "It must be a joke!" but he made a terrible face and answered, "Apparently this is not the moment for joking. Three or four of these bombs and Japan might be completely destroyed."

Isoko and Ichiro Hatano, *Mother and Son* (Boston: Houghton Mifflin, 1962), pp. 112–13, 116, 118–23, 124–26, 132–34.

Is it possible for such things to exist, and if they exist is it possible for people to use them? There are international agreements prohibiting the use of poison gas because it is inhuman; how can people use a bomb so much more terrible than gas?

I think Kinji is too ready to believe what his teacher tells him. We must take into account that Mr. Aoyama, Kinji's form master, is said to have been put on the blacklist because of his dangerous leftist ideas.

August 9, 1945

It seems that Kinji was right: the impossible did happen at Hiroshima on August 6th. They say that it is like hell there.

What is the reason for this war? Why is there so much hatred between men? I don't understand.

I realize now that the will of the individual means nothing; it can't do anything to change the course of events. I am so despondent that I don't even feel like going to school.

August 10, 1945

The Russians have declared war on us. People were looking to Russia as the only nation capable of mediating. That hope is gone now.

What will become of Japan?

The destruction of Hiroshima seems more total than was imagined at first. The voice of the radio announcer was choked with emotion.

Soon it will be Tokyo's turn, and then Yokohama's and then ours. It would be better if the whole thing were brought to an end at once.

August 12, 1945

They have dropped another unknown bomb—this time on Nagasaki.* According to the radio, the damage is not so extensive as at Hiroshima; but it is much more serious than after an ordinary raid. . . .

* In fact, the Nagasaki bomb fell on August 9, but conditions in Japan were so chaotic that the news took days to reach Ichiro in Suwa.

Was the Japanese army completely unaware that the other side had a weapon like this? In that case there is as wide a gap between Japan and the rest of the world as there was during the period of the Meiji Restoration, which we read about in our history books.

It was ludicrous to hope, even for a moment, that we could possibly win the war with bamboo spears. It was absurd to . . . believe that the legendary glories of our ancestors would renew themselves eternally.

It is true that we were taught that legend; but even without such indoctrination, the Japanese people believed instinctively that they would remain invulnerable until the end of time. Hiroshima and Nagasaki are opening [Japan's] eyes; its will to fight is melting away. But what can we do? The wishes of individuals don't really affect the course of a war. A nation may be made up of individuals, but war develops along lines different from those the majority would have chosen.

August 13, 1945

I think it is a crime to attack so many innocent people, most of whom have not even worked in the armaments factories. Christians maintain that a crime is forgiven if the criminal repents. This one will not be forgotten so easily.

The official communiqués are asking the people to unite in holy wrath against the cruelty of our enemies. I don't know whether unity is possible; but there is no doubt that young people like me are convinced of the wickedness of an enemy which acts contrary to all the laws of humanity.

This being so, we will never yield before such executioners; we would rather die. Certainly we will lose the war; but nevertheless we must not weaken.

August 15, 1945

It's unexpected, unbelievable! Yesterday, during the evening, my uncle arrived from Tokyo to tell us that the war is over. At first nobody believed him; the conflict had seemed interminable. But it is true. The war is over, suddenly and quickly.

It was the Emperor's decision; his wisdom is great! Once again I marvel at his power, and at his kindness toward his people.

The war is over and we have lost it. Yet I'm not terribly welcome the news wholeheartedly. I hate our unconditional surrender, to which death itself almost seems preferable.

On the one hand, I feel as though a window on one side of my heart were opening and letting in a breath of fresh air; on the other, I am despondent. What a contrast! Yesterday I was too happy to thank my uncle for coming to tell us the news, and today I can hardly bear to think of it.

What is going to be the outcome of it all? Will there really be peace and will we be able to stay quietly at home close to Mother? There is a rumor that, since Japan has lost, all the young men will be drafted into agriculture and all the girls will be sold to the enemy as prostitutes. I feel so bewildered that I cannot judge how much truth there is in all these rumors.

The only thing that is clear to me is that the war has ended before we are all dead. . . .

◆§Japan has been defeated. The enemy is victorious. But what of Ichiro? He had never shared in the unthinking hatred of his country's enemy. For one thing, Ichiro could see that his parents were disaffected long before the end of the war. In mid-July, well before the atom bombs fell, the Allies had begun to drop leaflets near Ichiro's home. Many thought the leaflets were poisoned.§◆

July 22, 1945

Mother . . . seems to think one shouldn't touch the leaflets. In her opinion, it is not impossible that they are poisoned, since they are dropped by enemy aircraft. I don't think so; if they were dropped for some evil purpose, they wouldn't advise people to evacuate certain areas which are going to be dangerous. Mother insists that we must be on our guard; but it doesn't seem like her at all. Usually she says that we must be more aware of goodness in other people and must view things as they are, without prejudice. Do these principles hold good only for the Japanese?

I don't think so. To take the present case, if the enemy is trying to save us from disaster, and the Japanese won't believe them, more shame to the Japanese. But even while I write, another me is whispering: "That's all very well, but it's the enemy that dropped the leaflets. They'll use any means to beat us." All the same, I prefer to believe that they acted from a sense of humanity.

I can easily imagine a boy, like me eager for justice, but probably a little older, flying over in his airplane and dropping the leaflets simply because he considered it cruel and unfair to hurt people who have nothing to do with the war. I see him, before his mission, giving his thoughts to his commanding officer; and the officer, from sympathy for Japan or perhaps because he had once been here, approving them. This is probably how they came to have mercy on the Japanese civilians and send the leaflets.

I try to cling to this idea even while everybody is shying away from the leaflets as though they were sent by the devil. Even if there is a bombing tomorrow, I would still prefer to hold on to this opinion.

On the day of the surrender, Ichiro and his mother resume their correspondence.

August 15, 1945

Dearest Mother,

So the war is over. I knew we were going to lose, but I didn't think it would be so soon. It hardly seems possible. It is like a dream. But the Emperor has spoken on the radio, so there can be no doubt.

The war is over. Yet, despite my feeling of relief, I cannot upset. Why, I wonder? Is it because I have so often heard Father and the others say it would be better for Japan to lose than continue fighting? Whatever the reason, I feel badly at not being able to share everybody else's unhappiness.

Mother, do you remember what happened at Aoyagi station? You certainly do. Some railwaymen were burning papers in the twilight. They didn't want them falling into the hands of American soldiers. As I watched that fire I felt my heart swelling with anger. But I didn't want to cry in front of you and the other people who were there. I looked ahead and saw Koike, a boy in the class above mine, slowly wandering off, his tattered satchel hanging from his shoulder and his hands in his pockets. He had a dejected look on his face and he was crying. At that moment I felt thoroughly ashamed.

Of course, the Koike family is not like ours, and I'm sure this boy himself never had the slightest idea that Japan might be beaten. But all the same, he and I are both Japanese. I should have been crying as he was. And, to tell you the truth, I wanted to.

Just as I was thinking about all this, I looked in your direction and was absolutely dumfounded; I expected your face to be sad; instead, it was calm and happy. You said: "Who's that boy, Ichiro?"

The tone of your voice was not sympathetic; it seemed almost contemptuous. I even thought I detected a certain amount of amusement. You have never surprised me as much as you did at that moment.

Mother, I know how much trouble Father has had during the war, and I know how much worry and gray hair this has given you. It even made me want to stop going to school and work in the fields in order to help you. So it does not surprise me that Father should be glad and that you should breathe more freely. But I don't think you should let other people see this. We are Japanese, like them, so we ought surely to be as sad as they are. I think those who cannot be sad themselves should at least identify themselves with the sadness around them. And yet, Mother, you said things like that today. What is more, when we returned home, you made fun of me and said I had put on a miserable face to imitate the other boy.

August 25, 1945

The Tokyo newspaper has published a report about the Hiroshima atom bomb. According to Truman, America spent $200 billion on this new weapon, and 185,000 men worked on it in a vast number of factories. The research and manufacture of the bomb were already under way before the beginning of the war—before Pearl Harbor. The Americans insist that they were forced to strike back after being surprised at Pearl Harbor.

But that's not true. America was already prepared. And then she did everything to get Japan into a difficult situation and force her into the war. In particular, she put a stranglehold on Japan by means of the blockade. And just as the starving mouse will eventually lash out at the cat, so Japan ended by attacking America.

At the time of Pearl Harbor I was naïve enough to be enthusiastic about our daring; then Father explained to me how dishonestly we had behaved and I was ashamed of my country. In many of the chronicles of our past there are similar examples of surprise attacks. . . . Father says that the Japanese have a natural tendency to consider the end result alone, without being too particular about the means they use to achieve it. That horrifies me.

Nevertheless, if, as Truman has said, America was working on the atom bomb as early as 1940 and in anticipation of the war, she is the one to be ashamed. Naïve and quick-tempered, the Japanese fell victim to America's strategy; and now they have been beaten by an enemy much stronger than themselves.

It is so disheartening, Mother. America says she puts peace before everything else; but to judge from what has happened, she is not to be trusted.

August 27, 1945

Mr. F., who works for a newspaper, showed me some photographs of Hiroshima. Just one chimney is left standing amid the ruins and scorched ground. How could a whole town disappear like that, in a few minutes?

There must have been many young schoolboys like us in Hiroshima. They were probably all killed; for not only were the factories razed to the ground but all the houses as well.

The Allied forces are about to land, and the other boys at school are afraid the Americans, since they had no hesitation about attacking defenseless people, will commit all sorts of atrocities.

When I said this to Father, he replied that the Americans were civilized people, so there was no danger. But wickedness is latent in civilized men; and isn't this the worst kind of wickedness?

Hiroshima and Nagasaki

◆§*Editor's Introduction:* The costs of the war for Japan were incalculable. Almost two million Japanese were killed, and many more injured. Japan lost her empire abroad and her economic machine at home.

Consider the following passage from the official U.S. Strategic Bombing Survey (December, 1946):

> By July, 1945, Japan's economic system had been shattered. Production of civilian goods was below the level of subsistence. Munitions output had been curtailed to less than half the wartime peak, a level that could not support sustained military operations against our opposing forces. The economic basis of Japanese resistance had been destroyed. This economic decay resulted from the sea-air blockade of the Japanese home islands and direct bombing attacks on industrial and urban-area targets.

The "urban-area targets" mentioned were cities, not factories or military positions within the cities, but the cities themselves. The report continues:

> The urban-area incendiary raids had profound repercussions on civilian morale and Japan's will to stay in the war. Sixty-six cities, virtually all those of economic significance were subjected to bombing raids and suffered destruction ranging from 25 to 90 per cent. Almost 50 per cent of the area of these cities was leveled.

Fire-bombing was employed "in the belief that the industrial results of urban-area attacks would be far more significant than they had been in Germany, because of the greater fire vulnerability of Japanese cities and the importance of small industry to Japanese

By Richard H. Minear.

This official Air Force photo suggests the extent of the damage inflicted by the atomic blast in the heart of Hiroshima. (Wide World Photos)

war production." The results described in the report were "achieved" *before* President Truman decided to use against Japan the atomic bomb our scientists had developed for use against Hitler.

For all the hardships he endured, Ichiro was fortunate in at least one sense: he was not himself a victim of atom-bombing. The residents of two Japanese cities were less fortunate: Hiroshima, bombed on August 6, and Nagasaki, on August 9, 1945.

The experts are sharply divided as to whether the atom bombs had any major effect in shortening the war, for Japan was already on the brink of defeat and total collapse. The experts are also divided as to whether the dropping of the two bombs was justifiable in terms of the laws of war.

How do you suppose it felt to be among the first victims of the atomic age?

ONE VICTIM OF the first atomic attack was a professor of history. When the bomb fell on Hiroshima, he was about three miles away from the blast center. Here are his words:

> A blinding . . . flash cut sharply across the sky. . . . I threw myself onto the ground . . . in a reflex movement. At the same moment as the flash, the skin over my body felt a burning heat. . . . [Then there was] a blank in time . . . dead silence . . . probably a few seconds . . . and then a . . . huge "boom" . . . like the rumbling of distant thunder. At the same time a violent rush of air pressed down my entire body. . . . Again there were some moments of blankness . . . then a complicated series of shattering noises. . . . I raised my head, facing the center of Hiroshima to the west. . . . [There I saw] an enormous mass of clouds . . . [which] spread and climbed rapidly . . . into the sky. Then its summit broke open and hung over horizontally. It took on the shape of . . . a monstrous mushroom with the lower part as its stem—it would be more accurate to call it the tail of a tornado. Beneath it more and more boiling clouds erupted and unfolded sideways. . . . The shape . . . the color . . . the light . . . were continuously shifting and changing.*

Many of the survivors of Hiroshima report that their first thought was that the bomb had fallen very near to them. Had that been the case, of course, they would not have survived. The professor of history was one of those who shared this illusion. He later composed this brief poem:

> Thinking a bomb must have fallen close to me,
> I looked up,
> But it was a pillar of fire three miles ahead.

When the professor discovered (to his surprise) that he was still able to move, he tried to find out what had happened. Where had the bomb fallen? What effect had it had?

> I climbed Hijiyama Hill and looked down [over Hiroshima]. I saw that Hiroshima had disappeared. . . . I was shocked by the sight. . . . What I felt then and still

* Quoted in Robert J. Lifton, *Death in Life* (New York: Random House, 1967), p. 19. Reprinted by permission. The following three quoted passages are also from Lifton—pp. 19, 29, and 27.

feel now I just can't explain with words. Of course I saw
many dreadful scenes after that—but that experience,
looking down and finding nothing left of Hiroshima—was
so shocking that I simply can't express what I felt. I could
see Koi [a suburb at the opposite end of the city] and a
few buildings standing. . . . But Hiroshima didn't exist—
that was mainly what I saw—Hiroshima just didn't exist.

The center of a city of 250,000 people had been devas-
tated. What of those people? A grocer, who suffered severe
burns himself, remembers what he saw in the immediate after-
math of the blast.

The appearance of people was . . . well, they all had
skin blackened by burns. . . . They had no hair because
their hair was burned, and at a glance you couldn't tell
whether you were looking at them from in front or in
back. . . . They held their arms bent [forward] like this
[he proceeded to demonstrate their position] . . . and
their skin—not only on their hands, but on their faces and
bodies too—hung down. . . . If there had been only one
or two such people . . . perhaps I would not have had
such a strong impression. But wherever I walked I met
these people. . . . Many of them died along the road—I
can still picture them in my mind—like walking ghosts.
. . . They didn't look like people of this world. . . . They
had a special way of walking—very slowly. . . . I myself
was one of them.

The bomb had robbed most of its victims of the capacity
to think clearly. There may have been little wild panic, but
there was a widespread sense of unreality and numbness. A
doctor recounts descriptions he heard:

Those who were able walked silently toward the suburbs
in the distant hills, their spirits broken, their initiative
gone. When asked whence they had come, they pointed
to the city and said, "That way"; and when asked where
they were going, pointed away from the city and said,
"This way." They were so broken and confused that they
moved and behaved like automatons.
Their reactions had astonished outsiders who reported with amazement the spectacle of long files of peo-

ple holding stolidly to a narrow rough path when close by was a smooth, easy road going in the same direction. The outsiders could not grasp the fact that they were witnessing the exodus of a people who walked in the realm of dreams.*

The atom bombs fell on Hiroshima and Nagasaki—on Japanese territory and on Japanese people. But the Japanese were not alone in their suffering. In a very real sense, we were all there. Together with the Japanese, we are all survivors of Hiroshima and Nagasaki. Hiroshima in particular has become a symbol to the world, a symbol whose relevance goes far beyond World War II and the Japanese. It has become the chief symbol of the nuclear age, of the holocaust that man's scientific genius has made possible. It has become a symbol of the potential consequence if man does not develop alternatives to war. It has become a symbol—one of the more recent in a long, long series—of man's inhumanity to man.

* Mikio Hachiya, *Hiroshima Diary*, translated by Warner Wells (Chapel Hill: University of North Carolina Press, 1955), pp. 54–55. Reprinted by permission.

Tojo's Testament

Editor's Introduction: Japan's suffering in the war was beyond measure. Almost two million Japanese died, and many more were injured. Japan's cities were flattened, and her economy came to a standstill.

Beyond these external and objective signs of damage were the less apparent internal scars. Losing a war that their leaders had assured them they would win came as a severe shock to most Japanese. After all, Japan had never before lost a war. Then there was the humiliation of having to surrender unconditionally, and the further humiliation of submitting to a military occupation of uncertain length (in fact, it lasted a relatively short time—seven years). Finally, the people suffered a loss of confidence—in their nation and in themselves. How are these losses to be measured? They were less visible than the dead, the wounded, and the flattened cities, but they were no less real.

The Allies, in particular the United States, contended that the Japanese leaders were international criminals, guilty of the crime of aggression and other conventional war crimes. They selected twenty-eight Japanese leaders to stand trial on these charges.

It did not seem to matter that aggression was not recognized as a crime in international law before 1945, let alone in 1928, when the planning for the supposed "aggressions" was thought to have begun. As late as 1944, the U.S. Government had stated that aggression was not criminal.

Nor did it seem to matter that the twenty-eight Japanese leaders were chosen in an arbitrary fashion. Consider the Emperor. The Allies chose not to accuse him of anything; yet he had been present

Sugamo isho hensankai, *Seiki no isho* (Tokyo, 1953), pp. 683–85. Translated by Richard H. Minear.

at many crucial meetings. If his ministers were almost uniformly considered guilty, why not the Emperor?

Nor did it matter that the trial itself was hardly fair. There were, for example, no Japanese judges and no neutral judges. All eleven judges came from the victor nations. Two of these judges understood neither English nor Japanese, the two official languages of the trial. One of the judges had spent the war as a prisoner of the Japanese: how could he judge Japanese "crimes" fairly? One of the judges was simply not present for one-fifth of the trial.

The rules stated that the judges would decide all issues by simple majority vote. One defendant was sentenced to die by a vote of six to five; six more were sentenced to die by votes of seven to four.

Unfair as it was, the trial went forward, and all twenty-five of the defendants who survived it were found guilty. Seven were hanged, sixteen were sentenced to life in prison, and two received lesser sentences.

The trial was aimed primarily at the Japanese people. That is, it was designed to teach them that their leaders were evil men and that their nation had pursued a policy that was criminal.

But as we have seen, Japan went to war in large part because her leaders had seen no acceptable alternative. We may argue that these leaders had far too narrow a conception of Japan's national interest, of what was "acceptable," but they thought they were acting in their nation's best interest.

Tojo Hideki, a general in the Imperial Japanese Army, had been Prime Minister at the time of the attack on Pearl Harbor and during most of the war. Found guilty at the Tokyo trial, he was condemned to death and hanged.

Throughout the trial and until his execution, Tojo conducted himself with great dignity. He admitted his responsibility for Japanese policy, and he answered forthrightly all questions asked him at the trial. He expressed only mild resentment of the fact that the trial was not a fair one. Six weeks elapsed between the day he learned his fate and the day of his execution. During that time he worried that he might catch a cold: he wanted above all to be in good health when he died.

The following is Tojo's testament as it was memorized by the Japanese prison chaplain. What kind of man do you think Tojo was? What was his attitude toward the United States?

WHEN I AS the man responsible at the time of the beginning of the war look at the scars of the lost war, I think truly heart-breaking thoughts. Although my death sentence is comforting to me as an individual, my responsibility to my country is not something I can atone for with my death. But as far as international crime is concerned, I asserted my innocence [at the trial]. Today I am of the same mind. It is only that I submitted in the face of force.

As for myself I am content to climb the scaffold bearing my responsibility toward the Japanese people. In this connection, it is truly a source of regret for me that I extended this responsibility to my colleagues and that the punishment extended even to subordinates. Toward the Emperor and toward the people it was an inexcusable thing I did, and I humbly beg forgiveness.

Properly speaking, the Japanese armed forces should act in accordance with the benevolent will of the Emperor; it was regrettable that one part of the armed forces went too far and was misunderstood by the world.

To the men lost in service in this war and to their survivors, I cannot make proper amends. From my heart I tender my apology.

As for the rights and wrongs of this tribunal, we must of course await the judgment of history. If the trial was designed to serve the cause of eternal peace, then would it not have been better to approach the issues with a slightly broader attitude? This trial was, after all, a political trial. It was only victors' justice.

The position of the emperor and his existence should not be changed. Concerning the form of the emperor's existence I venture to say nothing. His existence itself is absolutely essential. This is not only my feeling, but the feeling of many others. It is all too easy to forget an indebtedness [to the emperor] which is as omnipresent as the air and as extensive as the land.

The peoples of East Asia should forget recent events and cooperate in the future. The peoples of East Asia possess the right to live in this world just as do the other peoples; the fact that they are colored is indeed a gift of the gods. . . . Here I felt was something the various East Asian peoples could boast

Flanked by American Military Police, Tojo hears his sentence: death by hanging. (U.S. Army)

about. If through this war the right to existence of the East Asian peoples has begun to be understood, then that is to the good.

The Allies too should forget their exclusivist feelings and should proceed bearing in mind the common good. To the Americans who are now the actual rulers of Japan, I speak one word. I hope that somehow you do not alienate the feelings of the Japanese toward Americans. Further, I hope that the Japanese people will not be bolshevized [turned into Communists]. You must recognize the sincere intentions of the East Asian peoples and proceed to cooperate with them.

Indeed, this is the basic reason we lost the war: that we could not gain the cooperation of the other East Asian peoples. From now on Japan will probably exist under the protection of America, but what will the general situation in the Far East be like? It is barely three years after the end of the war, and the bolshevization of the Asian continent has already proceeded a long way.

When I think of what may follow, I am really full of anxiety. There could be no greater danger than that Japan should become a hotbed of bolshevism.

I am grateful now for the foodstuffs and other assistance Japan is receiving from America. However, should it develop that the man in the street feels that his own immediate hardships and the inflation and the shortage of food are caused by the presence in Japan of the American army, then that would be dangerous. In fact, there are those now spreading this kind

---

Japan Supports U.S. Education

The Sumitomo combine of mining, manufacturing, and banking announced today gifts of $3 million to promote Japanese–American cultural understanding. Two million dollars will go to Yale University (the largest gift Yale has ever received from a foreign source), and $1 million will go to the Japan Society of New York.

One of Sumitomo's rival combines, Mitsubishi Heavy Industries, presented Harvard University with $1 million last September. University officials in this country are hoping that other large Japanese corporations will come forward with similar gifts.

June 20, 1973

✿　　✿　　✿

The Japanese government today promised $10,000,000 in support of Japanese studies in American universities. Ten leading universities will receive $1,000,000 each. They include Harvard, Columbia, Chicago, Michigan, California (Berkeley), and Washington (Seattle).

August 7, 1973

of propaganda. Hence, I hope that the American army will not lose the hearts of the Japanese people.

❧*Editor's Postscript:* American leaders and the American people accepted at face value the verdict of the trial of Tojo and the other Japanese leaders. It seemed to confirm what American leaders had asserted during the war: that Japan had been criminally responsible for World War II in the Pacific, that Allied policy had been wise, and that the just cause had triumphed.

The unfairness of the trial itself went largely unrecognized. The Indian judge at the Tokyo trial stated his opinion that dropping the atom bombs was the greatest crime of the Pacific war, but no one seemed to notice. The French judge wrote that the trial was not a fair one, but again no one seemed to take note.

And so the trial ended in irony. The Allies set out to educate the Japanese people about their mistakes but wound up teaching themselves what they already believed—that the Japanese were wrong and the Allies right.❧

Two Constitutions

Editor's Introduction: Defeat in World War II brought many changes to Japan. First and foremost, it led to military occupation by the Americans. For seven years, from 1945 to 1952, Americans exercised ultimate authority in Japan.

The status of the Emperor was an immediate focus of American concern. Before and during the war, the Japanese government had made much of the Emperor's "godhood." The Emperor, it said, was the direct lineal descendant of the Shinto Sun Goddess; he was "the Sun Goddess living in the present." Loyalty to the Emperor therefore had powerful religious overtones.

Brought up to believe in the separation of church and state, Americans looked askance at this. How could democracy flourish under a "divine" Emperor? In response to American pressure, the Emperor inserted an extraordinary passage into his New Year's Day, 1946, address to the nation. The ties that bound the Japanese people to their Emperor, he said, did not depend on the false doctrine that the Emperor was divine.

This announcement was confusing to most Japanese. They had never considered the Emperor a "god" in the Western sense of that word. But there was little to do but go along.

A second change in the status of the Emperor was much more important. It affected his constitutional position and powers. Here is the Preamble and Article I of Japan's prewar constitution.

The Constitution of the Empire of Japan

Preamble

Having, by virtue of the glories of our Ancestors, ascended the Throne of a lineal succession unbroken for ages eternal; desiring to promote the welfare of, and to give development to the moral and intellectual faculties of Our beloved subjects, the very same that have been favoured with the benevolent care and affectionate vigilance of Our Ancestors; and hoping to maintain the prosperity of the State, in concert with Our people and with their support, We hereby promulgate, in pursuance of Our Imperial Rescript of the 12th day of the 10th month of the 14th year of Meiji [1881], a fundamental law of State, to exhibit the principles, by which We are to be guided in Our conduct, and to point out to what Our descendants and Our subjects and their descendants are forever to conform.

The rights of sovereignty of the State. We have inherited from Our Ancestors, and We shall bequeath them to Our descendants. Neither We nor they shall in future fail to wield them, in accordance with the provisions of the Constitution hereby granted.

We now declare to respect and protect the security of the rights and of the property of Our people, and to secure to them the complete enjoyment of the same, within the extent of the provisions of the present Constitution and of the law.

The Imperial Diet shall first be convoked for the 23rd year of Meiji [1890] and the time of its opening shall be the date when the present Constitution comes into force.

When in the future it may become necessary to amend any of the provisions of the present Constitution, We or Our successors shall assume the initiative right, and submit a project for the same to the Imperial Diet. The Imperial Diet shall pass its vote upon it, according to the conditions imposed by the present Constitution, and in no otherwise shall Our descendants or Our subjects be permitted to attempt any alteration thereof.

Our Ministers of State, on Our behalf, shall be held responsible for the carrying out of the present Constitution, and Our present and future subjects shall forever assume the duty of allegiance to the present Constitution.

Chapter I. The Emperor

Article I. The Empire of Japan shall be reigned over and governed by a line of Emperors unbroken for ages eternal.

⋙§A new constitution was issued in 1947, and this document remains in force today, without amendment. Written under heavy American pressure, it may, indeed, have been written *by* Americans. There were some Japanese who contended in 1947 that they could not understand the text of the new constitution (the *Japanese* text) because they did not know English.

Few people agree about the ultimate meaning of the changes embodied in the new Japanese Constitution. What real difference, after all, does an amendment to the American Constitution make in your life? Does your attitude toward the President of the United States depend on what is written in the Constitution? How much do you really know about the American Constitution?

In any case, however, it seems likely that the role of the Emperor in Japanese politics and thought has changed significantly. Here are the preamble and first article of Japan's current constitution.§⋙

The 1947 Constitution of Japan

Preamble

We, the Japanese people, acting through our duly elected representatives in the National Diet, determined that we shall secure for ourselves and our posterity the fruits of peaceful cooperation with all nations and the blessings of liberty throughout this land, and resolved that never again shall we be visited with the horrors of war through the action of government, do proclaim that sovereign power resides with the people and do firmly establish this Constitution. Government is a sacred trust of the people, the authority for which is derived from the people, the powers of which are exercised by the representatives of the people, and the benefits of which are enjoyed by the people. This is a universal principle of mankind upon which this Constitution is founded. We reject and revoke all constitutions, laws, ordinances, and rescripts in conflict herewith.

We, the Japanese people, desire peace for all time and are deeply conscious of the high ideals controlling human relationship, and we have determined to preserve our security and existence, trusting in the justice and faith of the peace-loving peoples of the world. We desire to occupy an honored place in an international society striving for the preservation of peace, and the banishment of tyranny and slavery, oppression and intolerance for all time from the earth. We recognize that all

The Imperial Family of Japan on New Year's Day, 1970. The Crown Prince stands behind the Emperor; his younger brother stands behind the Empress. (Consular General of Japan, N.Y.)

peoples of the world have the right to live in peace, free from fear and want.

We believe that no nation is responsible to itself alone, but that laws of political morality are universal; and that obedience to such laws is incumbent upon all nations who would sustain their own sovereignty and justify their sovereign relationship with other nations.

We, the Japanese people, pledge our national honor to accomplish these high ideals and purposes with all our resources.

Chapter I. The Emperor

Article 1. The Emperor shall be the symbol of the State and of the unity of the people, deriving his position from the will of the people with whom resides sovereign power.

Editor's Postscript: One fundamental goal of the American Occupation was to "demilitarize" Japan, to prevent Japan "from being a menace to the United States and the other countries of the Pacific area." Japan had threatened the Allies through her military might. Therefore, the reasoning went, remove Japan's military capability.

The result of this logic is Article 9 in the present Constitution, which reads as follows:

Aspiring sincerely to an international peace based on justice and order, the Japanese people forever renounce war as a sovereign right of the nation and the threat or use of force as means of settling international disputes.

In order to accomplish the aim of the preceding paragraph, land, sea, and air forces, as well as other war potential, will never be maintained. The right of belligerency of the state will not be recognized.

Voices were raised very soon in opposition to Article 9. What is a nation if it has no armed forces? Can it survive? Will it not always be dependent on powerful neighbors? Can you imagine the United States without a Pentagon? In fact, Japan today does maintain armed forces, called "Self-Defense Forces" to circumvent Article 9.

The Past Lives

❦*Editor's Introduction:* As we have seen, Article 9 of the present Japanese Constitution outlaws a standing army. Some Japanese have reacted strongly against this prohibition.

One of the most outspoken advocates of an armed Japan was Mishima Yukio, a highly respected novelist, playwright, and critic. Mishima felt that selfishness and greed had become the dominant values of postwar Japan. Life in Japan in the 1960s was affluent but without meaning. Rejecting this present, Mishima turned to the past, to the samurai values of physical fitness and absolute loyalty and devotion to the Emperor. Suicide in the ritual fashion of the samurai became for him the only clear expression of these selfless values.

In the following selection, Mishima explains why he established his own private army of one hundred men. He called this army the *Tate no kai*, or "shield society," and dedicated it to the defense, or shielding, of the Emperor. What does Mishima believe armed forces can do for modern Japan?❧

WE MUST REVIVE the warlike spirit of the samurai and take action even in the face of misunderstanding, silently, without words. Deep within me, I've always had the samurai's disdain for self-justification.

It is interesting to note that the concept of an irregular

Japan Interpreter, 7:1 (Winter, 1971), 77–78 (translated by Andrew Horvat), 73–77 (translated by Harris I. Martin). Excerpted and reprinted by permission.

army has completely disappeared in Japan. Since the beginning of our period of modernization in the last century, Japanese armies have in the main been composed of regular troops, and this has not changed with the present Self-Defense Forces. As a result Japan has not seen a militia in over a hundred years. Even during World War II, it was not until two months prior to defeat that the Diet passed the law establishing people's militias. The Japanese possess no other fighting skills except those learned in a regular army. They are unprepared in the face of the 20th Century's latest form of warfare: namely, guerilla combat.

Nevertheless, everyone I talked to laughed at my ideas of a popular militia, arguing that one just cannot form such groups in Japan. So I declared my determination to set up such an organization. And that is how the *Tate no kai* came into being.

In Japan, with the exception of Self-Defense Force veterans, there are no civilian youth outside the *Tate no kai* who have undergone even one month's military training. A similar situation might be unimaginable in European countries. Though we have only 100 members the military value of each is high. Should the necessity arise, each of these men could lead fifty. They are competent in rear guard operations and could engage in guerilla and intelligence activities.

Inferior as I am to the task, I am simply rekindling the dying embers of Japan's warrior spirit.

Our *Tate no kai* was nurtured by the Self-Defense Forces. In fact, one could say the Self-Defense Forces has been a father and an elder brother to us. Why, in order to repay that debt of gratitude, did we undertake this apparently ungrateful act? Looking back, we have been treated within the Self-Defense Forces as quasi-members, myself for four years, the students for three, and we have received training without any strings attached.

We love the Self-Defense Forces with all our heart. Dreaming of it as the "real Japan" which no longer exists outside its ranks, we have experienced within it the tears of men which have been unknown elsewhere since the end of the war. As comrades with a common spirit of patriotism, we have trained together on the plains of Fuji, and the sweat which has flowed from us is pure. Of these things there is not one iota of doubt.

For us, the Self-Defense Forces is our home and birthplace, and in the listless Japan of today it is the only place where we can breathe invigorating air. We cannot measure the affection we have received from our teachers and instructors. So all the more, then, how is it that we have dared to take this step? Though it may seem trite, I say it is because we love the Self-Defense Forces.

We have seen postwar Japan stumble into a spiritual vacuum, preoccupied only with its economic prosperity, unmindful of its national foundations, losing its national spirit, seeking trivialities without looking to fundamentals, and falling into makeshift expediency and hypocrisy. Gnashing our teeth, we have had to watch politics serve the glossing over of inconsistency, the protection of individual status, thirst for power, and hypocrisy. We have had to stand idly by while the policies and the future of the nation were entrusted to foreign powers, while the humiliation of our defeat was merely evaded and not effaced, and while the traditions of Japan were being desecrated by the Japanese themselves.

We dreamed that today the real Japan, the real Japanese, and the real [samurai] spirit exist nowhere else but in the Self-Defense Forces. . . .

Four years ago, on my own accord, I entered the Self-Defense Forces, and the next year I organized the *Tate no kai*. The basic idea of the *Tate no kai* lies simply in the determination to sacrifice our lives in order to make of the Self-Defense Forces, when it awakens, a national army, an honorable national army. . . .

We have waited four years. In the last year we waited fervently. We will wait no longer. There is no reason to wait for those who debase themselves. But we will wait for thirty

Mishima Yukio calls for an uprising of the Self-Defense Forces. Thirty minutes later, he was dead by his own hand. (UPI Photo)

more minutes, a last thirty minutes. We will rise together and together we will die for the right. We will die to return Japan to her true form. Is it right to protect life only to let the soul die? What kind of an army is it that has no higher value than life? Right now we will show you that there is a value higher than reverence for life.

It is neither freedom nor democracy. It is Japan. Japan, the country whose history and traditions we love. Is there no one who will die by hurling his body against the constitution which has mutilated her? If there is, let us rise together even

now, and let us die together. It is in the fervent hope that you
who are pure in spirit will once again be men and true
[samurai] that we have resorted to this act.

Editor's Postscript: As this selection indicates, Mishima was
willing to act on his convictions. On November 25, 1970, he and
four young companions stormed into the eastern headquarters of
the Self-Defense Forces and called for a revolt among the troops.
Mishima surely must have known that the response would be negative, and it was. Many of the servicemen who listened to Mishima's
impassioned speech that day responded with laughter. Mishima's
final act was to commit ritual suicide. He plunged a dagger into his
own abdomen, and one of his followers then beheaded him.

Mishima enjoyed great respect in Japan, and his death shocked
the Japanese people. But alive or dead, Mishima won few converts
to his ideals.

JAPANESE AID
FOR U.S. TRAINS

Three U.S. federal transport officials
arrived in Tokyo in late September to
study Japan's superexpress facilities and
seek technological co-operation in
building a new high-speed railroad
linking Washington, New York, and
Boston. . . . In addition . . . the officials
went along on a Shinkansen bullet train
trial run and inspected Shinkansen command posts.

Japan Report, Nov. 1, 1978

The Past Is Dead

ঌ*Editor's Introduction:* Mishima's death in 1970, dramatic though it was, seemed strangely irrelevant to the concerns of most Japanese. The Self-Defense Forces and Japanese society at large paid little attention. Life went on.

Mishima looked to the Japanese past for his values. But in Japan today there are many other sources of inspiration. The major works of all traditions—Western, Chinese, Indian—are available in Japanese translation. Indeed, Japanese students spend more time studying other countries than studying Japan.

Late in 1968, when most Japanese universities were shut down by student strikes, a group of more than 1,200 Japanese students responded to a public-opinion survey that asked which books had influenced them most deeply and which politicians they most admired. The students ranked Dostoevski's *Crime and Punishment* first and his *The Brothers Karamazov* third. Second was a Japanese novel written in the early twentieth century. Also among the top ten were *The Stranger,* by Albert Camus, Pearl Buck's *The Good Earth,* Tolstoy's *War and Peace,* and a German novel of protest. Twelve of the top twenty books were not Japanese but Russian, French, German, or American.

A similar pattern emerged from the answers about politicians the students respected. To be sure, a very large number of the students (more than 60% in the case of the most prestigious school, Tokyo University) asserted firmly that they respected no politician. Among those who did respond, the top four were John F. Kennedy, Lincoln, Lenin, and Churchill. The two most respected Japanese

Oe Kenzaburo, "The Right to Deny Japan," *Japan Quarterly,* 13:2 (April–June, 1966), 226–30. Reprinted by permission.

A young intellectual makes a point in a coffee-bar conversation. (Copyright by Doug Hurst)

politicians tied with Charles de Gaulle for *fifth* place. Also among the top twenty were Mao Tse-tung, Ho Chi Minh, Nehru, Gandhi, Che Guevara, Fidel Castro, Napoleon, Franklin Delano Roosevelt, and Robert F. Kennedy. Only four of the top twenty were Japanese.

It is clear that Mishima spoke for very few Japanese. Far more representative of the thinking of Japanese today is the novelist Oe Kenzaburō, creator of the character Bird, whom we have already encountered. Oe's typical hero is a modern man who happens to have been born in Japan. The dilemmas these heroes face are not exclusively Japanese.

Oe's concerns range widely. Not merely a novelist, he is a leading conservationist, and one of his books, *The Day the Whale Died*, is a plea for preservation of the Whale. Oe does not share Mishima's conviction that Japan today exists in a spiritual vacuum, nor does he share Mishima's romantic nationalism.

What does Japan mean to Oe?❧

AT HIROSHIMA AIRPORT, they sell oysters packed in barrels. You can leave Tokyo in the morning, meet a friend for lunch in Hiroshima, and have fresh oysters for dinner in Tokyo that night. Tokyo and Hiroshima television show the same Westerns, too. The Tokyo man and the Hiroshima man who discussed business during the day separate in the evening and then watch the same television program in Hiroshima and in Tokyo. There is nothing extraordinary about this, it has occurred to everyone. Japan today is linked from one corner to the other, unified, simplified. Time has whittled away at Japan until, in 1965, the entire country is no larger than any of the tiny villages you might have found . . . one hundred years ago.

But even you, who learn from watching television about everything that happens in this country, from the most important to the most trivial incident, even you must be ignorant of two deaths that occurred in Hiroshima during the past few weeks, the deaths of two young people. Yet the Japanese State was directly responsible for the first of these two related deaths and, as any Japanese with heart must feel, responsible for the second death too. The first death was attended by nausea and terrific pain in the joints, the second was the tranquil suicide of a young girl in utter despair.

There lived in Hiroshima a young man of 23 who was four years old when the Bomb fell. In his late teens, the boy's white cell count began running high, and he entered the Atomic Bomb Hospital. The specialists there saw immediately that he had leukemia. Ours is the age of space flight, yet leukemia, the so-called cancer of the blood, remains an untreatable, fatal disease. All that can be done is to halt temporarily the increase of white cells, to compel the disease to take a "summer vacation." In this case, the Hiroshima doctors managed to extend the vacation for a period of two years. But when the summer vacation is over, leukemia comes back to work and absolutely, unfalteringly, abducts its victim's life.

This particular young man expressed the desire to go to work while his temporary recovery lasted. The doctors, concealing the fact that he was in the grips of such a disease (no one would have hired him otherwise), found the youth a position at a printing company. And he did very well at his job. So well, in fact, that *Life* magazine carried an article about him, a cheerful young man dedicated to his work, which conveyed the impression of a healthy, new Hiroshima. Before long, he fell in love with a girl who worked in a music store, and they were soon engaged to be married.

Then the two-year period of grace expired, the agonizing nausea returned, and the young man went into the hospital again, where he died.

One .week after his death, the boy's fiancée appeared at the nurses' office at the Atomic Bomb Hospital; she had come to express her gratitude, and she brought with her a set of porcelain deer, one horned and powerful-looking, the other small and feminine. She was calm, apparently in perfect control of herself. The next morning, the girl was found dead from an overdose of sleeping pills, a suicide.

That same week, in Tokyo, the Japanese Government conferred the First Order of the Cordon Bleu on the man directly responsible for the bombing of Hiroshima. The Secretary-General of the Cabinet, grinning, had this to say:

"My house was gutted in the air raids too, but that's 20 years forgotten. Why shouldn't we present a medal to a soldier who bombed our cities during the war? In fact, the gesture represents the kind of open generosity that befits the people of a great nation."

To the *Life* readers in America who remember having seen a few years ago some pictures of a cheerful youth who had experienced the horrors of the Bomb, to those readers I would like to report what happened to that boy and his lover two years afterward. To the Secretary-General of the Cabinet I say that tragic, outrageous suffering is still resulting, right now, this very minute, from an incident *20 years forgotten.*

The youth who died of leukemia had a right to demand reparations from the Bomb which, if you will, sowed the seeds of disease in him when he was just a baby, to demand compensation from the war itself and from the State that brought about the War. None of the responsibility was his, yet 20 years later, as an individual, he became a victim of the war at the cost of his own life. If the State felt compelled to confer honors, it was to just such a young man that the medal of honor should have gone, though of course he would have refused it.

In fact, the young man did receive a medal, a real one, the suicide of the young girl who loved him and followed him in death. She was 20, born and raised after the war, and so she had nothing whatsoever to do with it. Yet she substituted for the State and, sacrificing her own life as an individual, as he had done, made of herself a medal for the young man. She, too, had the right to demand from the war and from the State reparations for the tragic loss of her fiancé, yet even at the moment of death, she did not criticize her country. Ten days apart, without a word to one another, the two lovers moved on to the land of death.

But this is not to say that these young lovers sacrificed themselves to their country because they loved it; quite the opposite must have been the truth. The boy was silent precisely because he knew that the State could do nothing for his leukemia, that bitter silence. The girl determined, how resolutely! that the entire world, including the nation called Japan, was not worth one dead young man, so she committed suicide. Foreknowing that the State and this great wide world could never afford her anything that could come even close to taking his place, she chose death. Turning her back on the State and on the world, she demonstrated with her own life that nothing so valuable as the dead boy would ever be discovered anywhere again. And what if a representative of the State and of the world at large had visited that Hiroshima music store and asked her not to die, *please, Miss, recognize that the State and the world, that all the people still living are worth more than that dead boy, and go on living;* most certainly she would have refused. *I'm finished with you* she would have said, *Japan has nothing to do with me now, not any more, and neither does the rest of the world, either.* When the young man died, the country called Japan, the entire second half of the twentieth century world, ceased to have any value for her whatsoever, she proved it beyond doubting with her suicide. And what a bitter taste it leaves in the mouth, this abject girl's heroic suicide.

And yet, with the radioactive material that sowed the seeds of death in that boy's body still playing the leading role in world government, what man on the face of this earth today can say YOU ARE MISTAKEN to a girl resolved to die? What can we do ourselves, save remain silent with bitter hearts?

Three teenagers chat on a Tokyo street. All were born long after 1945, when the atomic bombs fell and Japan surrendered. (Copyright by Doug Hurst)

Japan's postwar generation knows that it has the right to deny its own country, to say to Japan, not with the magnificent eloquence of the Hiroshima girl who committed suicide, nor in the voice of urgent defiance, but in tones appropriate to everyday life, to say *I'm through with you. I have nothing to do with you now.* The awareness of this right is the most beneficial wisdom the postwar democratic age possesses, but it is probably the most burdensome wisdom, too.

Before the war, when the Emperor's absolute authority cast a shadow in which all men stood, there must have been times when a patriotic man could not be sure whether his patriotism was merely the instinct of a slave in bondage to the State, or whether it was truly human will, a thing he had selected freely and for himself. The wills left behind on Edajima Island by the *kamikaze* pilots horrify because they are so clearly a mixture of this slavish instinct and individual, human volition.

While discovering patriotism may be extremely difficult for the postwar Japanese (difficult because, in times of peace more than in times of emergency, patriotism is in an inconspicuous state, commonplace as body temperature, which is not to say that it has been lost because it is not feverish. On the contrary, it continues to function in a normal, everyday way), we may assess our patriotism without reservations once we have managed to discover it for ourselves. This is because such patriotism has real value, has nothing to do with the predictable habits of a slave, because free men not bound to the State have willed it for themselves. And patriotism such as this must be a source of pride and pleasure, both for the State at which it is directed, and for the citizens who feel it. Our freedom reaches to the most fundamental levels; we are not bound to the State; the right to deny is ours—in this sense, the most beneficial wisdom of the postwar age.

Conversely, however, this awareness must be considered the most burdensome wisdom, a serious handicap, because the state of freedom is ever accompanied by uneasiness.

A good friend of mine once said to me:

"I got out of college six years ago and now I'm an assistant section chief at a pretty decent company; in other words, the most ordinary kind of citizen, the rank and file, and yet somehow I feel suspended, you know, apprehensive. And recently, I find myself saying 'I don't belong' all the time."

I don't belong? What did he mean by that, I asked.

"Just that, *I don't belong.* Like at breakfast, when I read the newspaper, and it says that some politicians who were ex-

pelled from the Communist Party have formed a new party—I
say to myself *I don't belong* to the Communist Party and *I
don't belong* to the splinter group either. I think if there were
ever a revolution I'd just wait around to see who had won.
Needless to say, I'm not a rightist and *I don't belong* to the
Conservative Party either. When the elections come up I vote
for some Independent who seems like a nice guy.

"In the train on the way to work I look at a weekly magazine, and there are pictures of a Sōka Gakkai rally and athletic
meet. [The *Sōka Gakkai* is a postwar Buddhist group with an
extraordinary zeal for spreading its gospel. It claims millions of
members.] And I think to myself, *I don't belong* to the Sōka
Gakkai. I have a feeling that the Independent I like in the
next elections will be forced out of the running by the Komeito
[the political organ of the Sōka Gakkai], and yet I have no
inclination to try and influence anyone else to vote for him.

"The magazine carries pictures of the Emperor too. But *I
don't belong* to the sentimental pyramid that installs the Imperial House at its apex.

"Even when I'm at work, I sense that *I don't belong* to my
company, not really, and when somebody drags me to a meeting where they show North Korean movies, I have the feeling
that *I don't belong* to Japan the way these new Koreans belong
to their country. I'm a Giants fan, too, but *I don't belong* to a
rooting club. What do you think? I mean, is this not belonging
complex something special to me? Anyway, there's no need to
worry, I'm not the kind of guy who gets more and more neu-
rotic until he has to hang himself—*I don't belong* to that club
either."

To hear my friend talk, you might think that he wanted
desperately to participate in some political party or religious
group, to belong to something, anything. Actually, such is not
the case. This particular form of freedom suits his temperament
well, and his disposition is probably shared by the average
Japanese citizenry in general, or at least by the "unbelonging"
rank and file, who far outnumber those Japanese who do belong. Though my friend feels vaguely apprehensive about his

state of freedom, at the same time he is perfectly aware that he has no desire for any state other than freedom. Force him to participate in something like the old-fashioned military system and he would immediately develop a "restrictions" complex.

Consequently, my friend, along with the millions of rank-and-file citizens just like him, has no choice but to select consciously this state of "unbelonging" as his own attitude. Now if, having redefined ourselves as "unbelongers," we rank-and-file citizens can maintain the stance that we represent, then there is no reason on earth why we should feel inferior to those who do belong. After all, the so-called "age of postwar democracy" was launched when we were liberated from a myriad restrictions belonging to the old Japanese order, and merged into a vast body of *petit bourgeois* who do not belong.

Two young cyclists flash the peace sign at an American photographer.
(Copyright by Doug Hurst)

The year 1965, which commemorates the one-hundredth anniversary of the Meiji Restoration, has been a year for discussing the rebirth of nationalism. And for the past several years now, there has been a tendency to intensify nationalism, sometimes innocently, sometimes in suspicious ways for dubious reasons. At any rate, a classical and orthodox version of prewar nationalism, the kind engendered in people who feel themselves essentially and inseparably bound to the State, has been revived, and is now asserting its authority. Those embracing this brand of nationalism conceive of themselves as a kind of organ which, were it cut away from the nation called Japan, would surely wither and die. But we members of the *unbelonging* rank and file, we millions, are not likely to grow ardent in support of any nationalism which requires us to sacrifice ourselves unreasonably, for we have experienced the sensation of being free of the State. Even if we should become infected, the fever would not last long. . . .

We rank-and-file citizens know that the right to deny Japan is ours and yet, except for a trifling number of international exceptions, we remain here. In other words, we elect to be Japanese as an act of individual and free will. And it is in the soil of this attitude that a new nationalism, different both from prewar nationalism and from its opposite, internationalism, will sink its roots and send up a mighty trunk.

I would like my attitude toward my country to reflect precisely this kind of nationalism. I want to remember the 20-year-old Japanese girl who not only denied Japan but bid farewell to the entire world. If there exists a state whose image could have inspired that devoted girl to go on living as a Japanese even after she had lost her fiancé, then that state, or one just like it, will be the flower that blossoms at the summit of the new nationalism.

An Asian Image of Japan, 1970

Editor's Introduction: Japanese nationalism has changed greatly since prewar days, but the basic economic dilemma remains. Japan is an industrialized giant in dire need of raw materials and export markets. Asia is the nearest source of both.

However, the resources and markets of Asia's largest country are closed to the Japanese. Mainland China is determined to establish its own economic independence, so Japan can look only to Southeast Asia. Roughly one third of Japan's imports come from this region, and roughly one third of Japan's exports go to this region.

In the following selection, a Japanese journalist reports on a trip to Thailand. What attitudes toward Japan does he find among the Thais? What questions about Japan does his experience in Thailand lead him to ask?

IN THAILAND, I heard all that I had expected to hear, and more. In fact, some of the things I heard were far beyond anything I could have imagined, so severe were the opinions.

"I think that the label 'economic animal,' recently thought up to describe Japanese, is apt because in business matters the Japanese are concerned only with making money. I very much hope that those Japanese who come to Thailand to work will learn to understand the Thai way of doing things and will, as

Kobayashi Keiji, "An Asian Image of Japan," *Japan Interpreter*, 7:2 (Spring, 1971), 129–37. Reprinted by permission.

a result, build industries that Thais can respect. Buddhist piety consists of just such behavior."

"Buddhist piety" is an expression Japanese do not often hear nowadays. . . . The man talking was Thailand's Minister of Economic Affairs, Bunchana Atthakor. He continued.

"Take, for example, the manufacture of irrigation pumps and small tractors. Although the Japanese work very hard to sell these items, should the machinery break down, they tell the customer that there are no spare parts and that he has to buy a new machine. Thanks to such practices. Thai farmers haven't got a chance; they can only become poorer and poorer until they die.". . .

I had been in Bangkok roughly a week. . . . The daily morning and evening rush hours, billboards which grace every view, and the noise . . . together, it presents the image of a little Tokyo. Visitors passing through the airport terminal are greeted by a huge Toyota ad, and the majority of roadside billboards on the way to the city center advertise Japanese goods.

If it were not for the special tropical quality of the heat, the magnificence of the temples one sees from time to time, and the disarray which Thai script presents to Japanese eyes, one would never know that he was in the capital of Thailand. The special characteristic of a "little Tokyo" lies in its total *lack* of any special characteristics. The markets are inundated by products made in Japan, and almost all taxi cabs are of Japanese manufacture. With the above impressions in mind, one can imagine the background for Minister Bunchana Atthakor's direct attack on Japan. . . .

THE PEAK OF UNPOPULARITY

Any research on Bangkok should begin with bargaining for a taxi ride. Taxis in Thailand are required by law to be equipped with meters, but they are rarely used. As one driver explained, "The officials are in cahoots with the manufacturers, and they make us buy the meters so *they* can line their pockets." Be that as it may, one must bargain separately for every destination, and a ride that only costs ten *bhats* one day can easily cost twenty the next. Japanese are presumed to be rich, so their fares tend to be especially high.

Whenever I stepped outside my hotel, the only one under Japanese management in the city, a number of pimp-like fellows would greet me in Japanese with "How about some souvenirs? Need a woman?" Japanese tourists are among their best customers. The Japanese-language school which recently opened its doors has been flooded with applications. The purpose of most of these applicants is not to gain an understanding of Japanese history and culture but, rather, to enlarge their employment opportunities through an ability to deal with Japanese customers.

With 6,000 Japanese residents, Bangkok has the largest Japanese population of any city in Southeast Asia. Furthermore, regardless of the season, a considerable number of tourists pass through the city, many using it as a stepping stone to Europe, India, or Indochina. And Japanese companies have moved into the local market in great strength.

According to information released by the Japanese Chamber of Commerce in Bangkok, as of late 1969, a total of 706 Japanese firms had received permission from the Thai Board of Investment (BOI) to engage in business in Thailand. The capital these companies pour into the Thai economy amounts to about $330,000,000. This sum accounts for 32 per cent of all foreign investment in Thailand; the United States takes second place, with 16 per cent, or half the Japanese total. Nine automobile companies, including Toyota, Nissan, Mitsubishi, and Honda, and eight manufacturers of electrical equipment, including Matsushita, Tōshiba, and Sanyō, are among the many big firms that have moved in. Japanese firms employ approximately 20,000 workers, most of them young and unskilled. Their average monthly salary is $32, which compares well with local pay levels. A policeman, for example, makes $25 a month. On the surface, such facts and figures indicate that Japanese enterprises are contributing considerably to Thai economic well-being, and yet the reputation of Japan has not risen one bit. . . .

DRAGGED INTO THE RED

Abe Yoshio, manager of Mitsui and Company, Thailand, Ltd., and head of the Japanese Chamber of Commerce, has been twice assigned to Thailand. He attributes anti-Japanese sentiment to the unfavorable balance of trade between Japan and that country.

For the Thais, the current imbalance in trade with Japan is no doubt one of their gravest problems and one that requires immediate solution. Thailand's trade has been in the red for the past few years, and the country has had to rely on America's special procurements for the Vietnam war in order to make ends meet.

. . . The problems inherent in the Thai-Japanese trade balance are matters of basic structure more than of figures and percentages. Thailand's principal export commodity is rice, and that item has been in excessive supply in Japan for some years. With the boom caused by American war procurements, on the other hand, Thai demand for Japanese consumer goods has been rapidly increasing. Given these conditions, there appears to be no way to remedy the imbalances in Japanese-Thai trade except perhaps through drastic expansion of Japanese aid to Thailand. . . .

PROBLEMS OF RACE AND CORRUPTION

According to some, a [crass, materialistic] life style is responsible for the generally low regard in which the Japanese have come to be held. Certainly, there are many Japanese in Bangkok whose comparatively high incomes ($500 and more per month) permit them such luxuries, unimaginable in Tokyo, as owning a fine house and keeping a maid and a chauffeur. At a *sushi* parlor operated by a hotel, slices of fresh tuna, flown in especially from Tokyo, are available at the price of two for $25, or the equivalent of a factory girl's monthly earnings. Those who are accustomed to expense-account spending on the Ginza [Tokyo's business district] think nothing of stuffing themselves with such delicacies. But such behavior can easily arouse the antagonism of the local people. . . .

Of all my informants in Thailand, it was S. who gave the most convincing answers to my questions. S. was well versed in both Thai and Japanese affairs. From language training to graduate school, he had spent a total of seven years at a Japanese university. As such he would have been an appropriate critic, but as he was section chief in a Japanese company he was somewhat reluctant to speak out. The following is a summary of some of the shortcomings he attributed to Japanese firms in Thailand: (1) Japanese companies pay higher wages to European- and American-educated employees than to those who have been educated in Japan. With bad companies the difference can amount to as much as $50. (2) The number of Japanese employees in a Japanese firm never decreases. Thus avenues of promotion are closed to local people. For example, an American or European firm may send out ten people to set up a company, but within five years only two or three will remain. With Japanese firms, despite the frequent transfers, the total number of Japanese employees remains the same. (3) The Japanese make no effort to understand the local mentality. Instead they always measure things according to their own standards.

I found out later that these deficiencies held true for Japanese firms in other parts of Southeast Asia as well. Finally, S. emphasized Thai nationalism: 70 per cent of all cars, buses, and trucks in that country are "made in Japan." Appliances, textiles, and other goods of Japanese manufacture are found in every city. The university clock tower is Seiko, while a sign on the pedestrian overpass advertises its donor, a Japanese firm. Can Thais be blamed if, surrounded by these nagging billboards and merchandise, they fear an economic takeover by Japan? . . .

DIFFERING OUTLOOKS ON LIFE

I have tried to explain some of the reasons behind anti-Japa-

nese feeling in Thailand. Most of my explanations are at least
partially valid, but I feel there is some other, more basic reason for that antagonism. It is the different sense of values
which evolved from different religious and cultural back-
grounds. For example, the Buddhism of Thailand belongs to
the Hinayana tradition. It is considered only natural that the
rich should give to the poor. To the Thai way of thinking, to
have enough to give is enough to make one happy. While driv-
ing to work one day, a Japanese executive of a joint-venture
corporation hit a local pedicab. The blame lay quite obviously
with the pedicab driver, who had not exercised due care and
attention while crossing the street. The policeman investigat-
ing the accident ordered the executive to compensate the pedicab driver: "As you are rich you won't have any problem getting
your automobile repaired. This man is poor. He has no money
to fix his pedicab. Therefore you must pay him the money to
do so." The executive explained to me, "This is not an example
of ill-feeling toward Japanese. They really believe that that
was the only correct decision."

Japanese would voice no objections if the donor of a
pedestrian overpass erected an advertising sign on his gift. Not
the Thais. They would probably say that the donor had derived
enough merit by giving the overpass and should covet nothing
more. . . .

On the last day of my visit to Bangkok, I got up early to
take a look around the famous floating market. The tour consisted only of a Korean couple from Tokyo and myself. Along
the way the guide bought a bunch of bananas for a mere 25¢.
The taste was beyond comparison with any sold in Tokyo.

The residents of the market did not mind our curious
looks; perhaps used to being stared at by tourists, they carried
on their usual business. The river, or rather the water, touched
every aspect of their lives. These people did their laundry, prepared their food, and washed their faces in this yellowish water. They even bathed in it. "What a terrible life!" the Korean
woman said, knitting her eyebrows. She looked at me, hoping I
would confirm her opinion.

On the spur of the moment I answered, "Really? They may be much happier with their lot than we with ours." My reply was prompted by the words of a Japanese girl I had met in Vientiane. She was living with a Laotian family in order to learn the language. She had come to question the meaning of Japanese economic aid. "Should we really be trying to involve them in our economic way of life? They may appear on the edge of poverty, but they live happily with what they have."

The Korean woman seemed a little startled by my retort. And then, after a short interval, in her perfectly fluent Japanese, she gave that neither affirmative nor negative reply, "I wonder."

Japanese Premier Meets Thai Students

BANGKOK, Thailand—Premier Tanaka of Japan met here today with representatives of students who had been denouncing his visit as symptomatic of "economic imperialism."

Chants in English of "Jap, go home!" were heard yesterday shortly after he arrived. They came during a roaring demonstration in downtown Bangkok by more than 2,000 students, who held forth from noon well into the evening.

New York Times, January 11, 1974